GOD OR GODLESS?

GOD OR GODLESS?

ONE ATHEIST. ONE CHRISTIAN.
TWENTY CONTROVERSIAL QUESTIONS.

JOHN W. LOFTUS
RANDAL RAUSER

BakerBooks

a division of Baker Publishing Group
Grand Rapids, Michigan

© 2013 by John W. Loftus and Randal Rauser

Published by Baker Books
a division of Baker Publishing Group
P.O. Box 6287, Grand Rapids, MI 49516-6287
www.bakerbooks.com

Printed in the United States of America

Library of Congress Cataloging-in-Publication Data is on file at the Library of Congress, Washington, DC.

ISBN 978-0-8010-1528-1

The internet addresses, email addresses, and phone numbers in this book are accurate at the time of publication. They are provided as a resource. Baker Publishing Group does not endorse them or vouch for their content or permanence.

Published in association with the Books & Such Literary Agency, 52 Mission Circle, Suite 122, PMB 170, Santa Rosa, CA 95409-7953.

13 14 15 16 17 18 19   7 6 5 4 3 2 1

John

I dedicate this book to the various respectful bloggers on both sides of this debate who have fine-tuned my understanding of the issues.

Randal

In 2003 my *doktorvater* Colin Gunton, theological mentor and personal friend, passed away unexpectedly just months after my thesis defense. Colin believed theology should be presented unapologetically even as it engages with a skeptical culture. I trust he would have been pleased with the spirit of these debates, and I dedicate this book to his memory.

Contents

Acknowledgments   9

An Irreverent, Interesting, and Somewhat Informative
Introduction   11

1. If There Is No God, Then Life Has No Meaning   13

2. The Biblical Concept of God Evolved from Polytheism
   to Monotheism   21

3. If There Is No God, Then Everything Is Permitted   29

4. The Biblical God Required Child Sacrifices for His
   Pleasure   37

5. Science Is No Substitute for Religion   45

6. The Biblical God Commanded Genocide   53

7. God Is the Best Explanation of the Whole Shebang   61

8. The Biblical God Does Not Care Much about Slaves   69

9. If There Is No God, Then We Don't Know
   Anything   77

10. The Biblical God Does Not Care Much about
    Women   85

11. Love Is a Many Splendored Thing, but Only if God Exists   93

12. The Biblical God Does Not Care Much about Animals   101

13. Everybody Has Faith   109

14. The Biblical God Is Ignorant about Science   117

15. God Is Found in the Majesty of the Hallelujah Chorus   125

16. The Biblical God Is Ignorant about the Future   133

17. God Best Explains the Miracles in People's Lives   141

18. The Biblical God Is an Incompetent Creator   149

19. Jesus Was Resurrected, So Who Do You Think Raised Him?   157

20. The Biblical God Is an Incompetent Redeemer   165

The Last Word   173

Recommended Readings   183

Notes   197

Acknowledgments

John thanks . . .

When I first went online to discuss my doubts in 2005, I found a particular evangelical forum that treated me with disdain and vitriol simply because I disagreed. I knew most Christians were not like this, but this group poured gasoline on the fires of my passion like nothing else. They provoked me to go for the jugular vein of a faith that could be used to justify their treatment of people like me. If it hadn't been for them, I probably would have moved on with my life. So I want to acknowledge them for helping to motivate me.

Randal thanks . . .

First, I'd like to express my gratitude to my wife, Jasper, and daughter, Jamie, for their support and patience on this and every other writing project in which I am engaged. Second, I'd like to thank Janet Grant, my agent, for her commitment to finding *God or Godless* the right publisher. Finally, I'd like to thank my opponent, John W. Loftus. I appreciate the fact that John is a very capable defender of atheism who argues his case with knowledge and passion. I also appreciate his ability to distinguish arguments from persons and thus maintain cordial relations even in the midst of deep disagreement. For these reasons I am especially grateful for John's participation in these debates.

An Irreverent, Interesting, and Somewhat Informative Introduction

We (John and Randal) enjoy formal philosophical debates about big and important issues, and they don't come any bigger or more important than the question of whether God exists. But as much as we love formal philosophical debates, they have their drawbacks too. For one thing, they often take way too much time. (Two or three hours in a stuffy lecture theater is a tax on anyone's stamina.) For another, they often are a bit *too* formal (dare we say *anal-retentive*?). And finally, they are often fixated on a narrow set of questions that, while important, have been asked a million times before, like "Does God exist?" and "Did Jesus rise from the dead?" Important and interesting questions to be sure, but there are different ways to slice the pie, and we think it is high time to approach from some fresh angles the same old debate over whether God exists.

With all this in mind, we wrote *God or Godless?* as a rather immodest attempt to address all that is lacking in the standard discussions. To kick things off, each of us chose ten debate statements in which the one who made the choice argued the affirmative while leaving the opponent scrambling to establish a case for the negative. I (Randal the Christian) seek through these debates to make a case for going with God, while I (John the atheist) aim to make the case for going Godless. With that basic formula in mind, we then tailored our twenty exchanges to address the weaknesses in the standard debates. First, we've cut down the length. Forget hours of ponderous argument, tortured rebuttal, and meticulous cross-examination: in each of our debates we were restricted to opening statements of about 800 words, rebuttals of about 150 words, and closing statements of a meager 50 words. As a result we managed to touch on all the main issues on the topic in question in a breezy debate that can be read in about twenty minutes. Second, we bypassed most of the traditional questions and topics to make way for some new angles and issues. And finally, so far as the formalism of academic discourse is concerned, let's just say that we weren't wearing neckties when we wrote this book. We purposely sought to keep the mood light, and we left the official timekeeper at home.

Before we begin, we'd like to point out one more thing. There is a handy bibliography at the end of the book that provides our suggested readings for each debate. Yes, we admit that we cannot exhaust each of these topics in twenty minutes. Our hope is that you view these brief debates not as the last word on any issue but rather as an invitation to further reading, discussion, and debate.

So without further ado, we turn to the task at hand. Pull up a comfortable chair by a roaring fire, don your most intelligent-looking reading glasses, pour yourself a cup of coffee or a snifter of port, and join us in addressing the grandest of questions: Should I go with God or Godless?

◀ 1 ▶

If There Is No God, Then Life Has No Meaning

Arguing the Affirmative: **RANDAL THE CHRISTIAN**

Arguing the Negative: **JOHN THE ATHEIST**

▶ Randal's Opening Statement

Nancy Sinatra topped the pop music charts in 1966 with her immortal, quasi-feminist hit, "These Boots Are Made for Walking." With those memorable lyrics, Sinatra educated an entire generation in the perambulatory purpose of go-go boots. If go-go boots were designed for a purpose, then it stands to reason that you can *fail* to use them for their intended purpose. For instance, the person who uses them as a utensil to spread Cheez Whiz on toast or as a drinking vessel for a pint of ale thereby *misuses* them. Though a person can sometimes effectively use an object intended for one purpose for a different purpose—for instance, a hammer can double as a handy paperweight—it should come as no surprise that generally speaking the best uses for objects are those for which they were originally designed. Typically it is not wise to flout the intended purposes of the original designer.

Now let's shift our gaze from our sparkling pair of go-go boots to a plain rock—perhaps a misshapen piece of shale lying in a valley bottom. Unlike the boot, the rock wasn't created for any purpose. It was just churned out through the deaf, dumb, and blind geologic processes that formed the earth. Consequently it is not *for* anything. It just *is*. Since it was not created for any specific purpose, then I can't *misuse* it. On the contrary, I simply decide to what use I may put it (if any), and I proceed accordingly. Maybe I decide to use the rock to cut a piece of rope while my companion opts to use it as a hammer to drive his tent peg into the ground. (More soberly, perhaps he uses it as a hammer to drive *me* into the ground.) I can hardly protest that my companion is *misusing* the rock since it wasn't created for any purpose to begin with. We're both free to use it however we choose. So a rock is very different from a boot. A go-go boot that is only used to spread Cheez Whiz (or still worse, that lies unused, forgotten, and molding in a dingy basement) is *not* a go-go boot that has fulfilled the perambulatory ends for which it was created. But a rock can neither achieve nor fail to achieve its purpose since the rock never had a created purpose to begin with.

As you probably have guessed, this talk of boots and rocks is merely prefatory to the talk of something else: persons. Sinatra's boots clearly have a purpose, but does she? Do any of us? Do human beings have objective purposes written into us by a designer or not? In other words, are we more like go-go boots—objects created by a mind for a particular purpose or end? Or are we more like rocks—objects randomly created with no objective purpose at all? This is a hugely important question to answer, for if we are like the boots, then we too can fail to achieve the purpose(s) for which we were created. But if we are like the rock, then we have no purpose apart from whatever *we* may choose to do or be, just like a rock has no purpose except for the arbitrary uses to which people put it.

I think a little reflection strongly disposes us against a lowly *rock view* of human beings. Surely we are not merely like rocks—objects that can be arbitrarily appropriated to any purposes we (or anyone else) may happen to desire. My evidence for this claim? We recognize that of all the various life goals people can set for themselves, some of those goals are inherently preferable to others. So, for instance, a person can set as his or her life goal to become a prolific prostitute serial killer like the mythical Molly Hatchet, or one can aim to help the poor like the blessedly not-mythical Mother Teresa. Surely the latter option is objectively preferable to the former; it is a better use of the life given.

The life lived by Mother Teresa is objectively preferable to that of Molly Hatchet because she more closely approximates the intended created end of a human being. And that means there are objective facts that guide the proper living of a human life as surely as there are facts that guide the proper wearing of go-go boots. Our lives can be lived well and they can be lived terribly. We all intuitively recognize that there are right ends and wrong ends to which we can put our life just as there are right ends and wrong ends to which we can put our go-go boots. And the further away we are from the intended purpose, the worse off we will be. Thus our lives are more like go-go boots than rocks; we too were designed for a particular end. But for what were we created? The answer to that question depends on how we answer another: *By whom* were we created?

▶ John's Opening Statement

Let's say someone locked up ten of us in a house with fully paid utilities and the necessities of life. There is no way for us to escape. We don't know who did this or why we were locked up together. We aren't told what to do while here. We don't even know if or when we'll be set free. As far as we can tell, we were chosen at random to be here together for no reason at all. Now what?

I'll tell you what I would do. I would find things to occupy my time for starters. And the more productive these activities are, the better. I would get to know the others by engaging in meaningful conversation, because people are interesting to me. I would do things with the others too. I would find activities we could do together, like playing lots of games, or working to keep the house clean, or seeing how many different kinds of meals we could make from the ingredients given us. If I were single, I might try to see if I could hook up with an interesting and attractive girl for sex and close companionship. If there was someone depressed or hurting in some way, I would try to help him or her. I would try to find as much meaning for my existence in that situation as I could, for it would give me plea-sure—holistic pleasure. I would be my own meaning maker. Having purpose and meaning makes human existence worth living, so that's what I would do. I can't do otherwise.

Living in that house is like living in this world. Analogies break down somewhere, of course, since there is no deity who placed us in this world. Still, we didn't ask to exist, nor have we been told why we are here. It's up to us to occupy our time with meaningful work and meaningful relationships. There is no other alternative. We must create meaning and purpose. No one else will do it. So why not make the best of our situation and live life to the fullest, accomplishing great things by seeing what we can do with our lives for the common good? There is nothing problematic about this at all. Is there something we can accomplish that may initially seem beyond our capabili-ties? There is purpose in that! Can we do something better than others? Can we accomplish nice things for people? Can we be remembered long after we die by the people with whom we came in contact? We set goals and seek to achieve them in life. There are short-term ones and long-term ones. They alone give us meaning and purpose.

That some people choose abusive, self-destructive purposes for their lives is sad, but that's exactly what they are doing, and it's a good reason not to do likewise.

This existence of ours may be pointless from the perspective of a million years. But why should that matter to us at all? Our lives will still matter to our family, friends, and the common good. Does the fact that I care for them mean anything to the ones I love? Does it mean anything to me that they care for me? The answer is obvious. Yes, unequivocally yes. So why should we value the distant future over the present? Our present life is all we have. It just doesn't matter *now* that in a million years nothing we do matters.

The delusional belief that what we do matters for all of eternity provides a false hope. Such a false hope falls under the Marxist critique that religion acts like a drug to numb us from the pain of injustice on earth through hope of a heaven in the afterlife. Having eyes on a heaven in the sky causes believers to be no earthly good. In fact, the hope of an afterlife devalues human life. Who really cares if people die when we go to war? The righteous will go to heaven. So let's go to war. What does it matter if we abuse the environment? This earth is not our eternal home. What does it really matter that a tsunami wiped out a quarter of a million people? God will reward believers with eternal life. "The poor you will always have with you," Jesus reportedly said (Matt. 26:11). So don't be too concerned that twenty-three thousand people starve to death every single day.

Only neo-humanistic purposes can help us.

▶ Randal's Rebuttal

John's illustration is telling. He says that once we are locked in the house (a metaphor for life) our first task is to find a way to occupy our time. *That's it*? Is our overarching goal merely to keep ourselves busy? And how should we do that? John suggests helping others because "it would give me pleasure." That's fine if you happen to get your jollies from helping others, but what about those who find pleasure in *hurting* others? Is that okay too? John's answer is not reassuring; since our existence is "pointless" anyway, he can only say that "we must create meaning and purpose." So I guess hurting others *is* okay then? As his final act, John tries desperately to drag me down with him by claiming that religion offers false hope. This is an ironic objection, for if John is correct that meaning is invented, then a religious construction is no worse than any other. Unfortunately for John, his caricature bears no resemblance to the Christian belief that God is restoring creation (Rom. 8:20–21; Col. 1:20) and has invited us to find our life's purpose in working for his peaceable kingdom. Far from mere time filling, Christianity offers a real, meaningful life.

▶ **John's Rebuttal**

Neither Sinatra's boots nor rocks nor human beings were created by a deity for any purpose. Unlike boots and rocks though, we have evolved to be our own meaning makers. We were thrust into this world and must now make the best of this life. We cannot do otherwise.

Let's talk about what we need to have a happy and fulfilling life. We need people. No one is an island. Social ostracism is painful, as is poverty, illness, or a life lived in prison. It's doubtful any reasonable person prefers these things to having friends, wealth, food, health, and freedom. So in order to gain these benefits a person must have a kind and trustworthy character, earn his or her keep, stay healthy and fit, and obey the law. People who pursue risky behaviors or sick fantasies will eventually lose their freedom; so reasonable people don't chase after those things.

Since we cannot turn on and off what we value like a faucet, we must sometimes act contrary to our immediate self-interests for an overall life plan that includes friendship, love, and worth.

Holistic happiness is its own reward. That is all the meaning we need in life.

▶ Randal's Closing Statement

John believes that we are "our own meaning makers." So what about Molly Hatchet? I assume John considers the life of a prostitute serial killer *sick*, but why isn't that just his subjective opinion? If human lives are objectively purposeless, then there isn't an objectively wrong way to live a life.

▶ John's Closing Statement

Once locked inside the house of life we must get along if we want the benefits of a life worthy to be lived, and that means mutual cooperation. Those who refuse we ostracize. Those who choose to hurt others will eventually be caught and banished from society in jail.

◄ 2 ►

The Biblical Concept of God Evolved from Polytheism to Monotheism

Arguing the Affirmative: **JOHN THE ATHEIST**

Arguing the Negative: **RANDAL THE CHRISTIAN**

► John's Opening Statement

Biblical scholars long ago acknowledged that many of the texts in the Bible were created or edited down through the centuries to reflect later hindsight historical perspectives. The editors did this to strengthen political power by consolidating the rival religious factions within a kingdom. In an ancient era when the masses were illiterate, few would be the wiser, and where criticizing the kings and priests in power would get you killed, the political powers that existed had it easy. Just create or rewrite history. The evidence for this is overwhelming in the Bible.

These editors didn't always do their job successfully because they didn't have access to all the texts. They were also written on scrolls, making it difficult to check for contradictions. But they didn't need to make it all consistent since they were the ones choosing what to read to the people. A key moment in time was during the reign of King Josiah in the seventh century BC (ca. 641–609) when the long-neglected book of Law was found (see 2 Kings 22–23). Scholars think that instead of *finding* the Law, this is when it was actually compiled and much of it written. Josiah instituted religious reforms to keep a crumbling kingdom together in the midst of a period of political turmoil when Israel was caught in the middle of a conflict between two great empires. This helps explain why Josiah's editors tell us the Passover meal was not celebrated for hundreds of years before their time (2 Kings 23:21–23). More likely, it was probably first celebrated during these reforms.

A case in point is that Hebrew understandings of the biblical God Yahweh evolved over time from a Canaanite deity to the head of a pantheon of deities, later to be declared the only God of the cosmos in Isaiah (Isa. 43:10; 44:24).

But there are many biblical texts, including archaeological discoveries, that lead us to think differently. In Genesis 1:26 we find God (i.e., *Elohim*—a plural word meaning "gods") speaking collectively as a council, saying, "Let us make mankind in our image" (see also Gen. 11:7). So already we have a plurality of gods if we read this verse properly rather than with hindsight Christian trinitarian assumptions foreign to the text. The Canaanite god *El* (or *Elyon*), who was the head of the pantheon, gave the people of Israel to Yahweh to rule over. We read in Deuteronomy 32:8–9 this: "When Elyon divided the nations, when he separated the sons of Adam, he established the borders of the nations according to the number of the gods. Yahweh's portion was his people, Jacob his allotted inheritance." This better translation is Thom Stark's based upon the Dead Sea Scrolls (4QDeut^q), which pre-date our current *Masoretic Text* by a thousand years.[1] References to a divine council all assume the existence of other gods (1 Kings 22:19–22). Psalm 82:1 reads: "God presides in the great assembly; he renders judgment among the gods." There were also many "sons of God" (Gen. 6:2 NIV; Job 1:6; Job 38:7 RSV; Psalm 29:1).

These earlier biblical texts did not deny the existence of other gods and their children (Judg. 11:24; Pss. 82:6; 89:7; 95:3; 97:7). Even the first of the Ten Commandments acknowledges the existence of other gods: "You shall have no other gods before me" (Exod. 20:3). It just forbids worshiping them. The point of these texts is that since the Israelites were Yahweh's people, they should worship him alone.

What we see here is no different than what we find in other cultures connected through the trade route of the Fertile Crescent, whose deities were polytheistic families of gods with a supreme one ruling over them. There was Marduk, the patron deity of Babylonia, and Ra, the father of the Egyptian gods; and in Canaanite society there was El or Elyon, the god most high, who was later superseded by Baal, the lord of heaven.

If the Canaanite culture and its god Baal had continued to exist down through the centuries as Yahweh has within Judeo-Christian cultures, then Baal would have been transformed into a monotheistic god. He would have progressively gained many of the same attributes Christians have heaped on Yahweh, and with the same philosophical sophistication. Then Baal worshipers would be the ones talking about progressive revelation and asking me why Baal could not reveal himself any way he chooses to do so.

No one believes in Baal today. Why should we believe in Yahweh?

▶ **Randal's Opening Statement**

Five hundred years ago virtually all educated people in the West believed that the earth was the fixed center of the universe. *Terra firma* was the center of action while the poor sun was a mere satellite revolving around our proud, immovable station. We now know that this picture was, to say the least, a bit off. To begin with, our grasp of the size differential was all wrong. It now turns out that the earth is (if you'll excuse the expression) the equivalent of a pimple on the sun's fiery bottom. And as for fixed points, the only thing really fixed is the sun's inescapable gravitational grip upon our tiny rock that has kept it spinning in lockstep for billions of years. To sum up, a rudimentary survey of our astronomical advances over the last few hundred years supports the fact that people's scientific concept of the universe evolved from geocentrism (earth-centered) to heliocentrism (sun-centered).

The shift from viewing the earth as the grand, fixed center of the universe to the lowly third rock out from the sun occurred through innumerable small steps and the occasional jolting leap due to the hard work of countless scientists like Copernicus, Galileo, and Kepler. We need not bother ourselves with the intricacies of that history here, for the main point is simply this: *Nobody* thinks that we ought to reject heliocentrism because we once believed geocentrism. To suggest such a thing would be positively absurd.

Now we are in a place to discuss our topic: "the biblical concept of God evolved from polytheism to monotheism." I don't actually disagree with this proposition. Instead, I disagree with the implications one may try to draw from it. Allow me to explain. It is true that the biblical conception of God emerged out of a polytheistic culture that only later converged on the austere doctrine of monotheism. In the ancient Near Eastern milieu in which God first called Abram out of Ur, everybody was polytheistic, so it is no surprise that Abram was as well. His move was not to monotheism but rather to *monolatry*—the worship of one God in the midst of many. Centuries later at the exodus from Egypt, the Hebrew understanding developed again. As Yahweh soundly defeated each one of the Egyptian gods, the Hebrews moved from mere *monolatry* to *henotheism*—the view that one God is far superior to all other gods.

By the time we get to the writing of Isaiah some centuries later, the Hebrew understanding had developed again. God was then understood to be so far superior to other beings that he was in a class by himself while all these other beings were demoted to mere creatures: "I am the first and I am the last; apart from me there is no God" (Isa. 44:6).

So to sum up, it took several centuries for the Israelites to move from polytheism to monotheism just as it took Western astronomers several centuries to move from geocentrism to heliocentrism. If you don't reject the results of astronomy because it reveals a developmental history, why for that reason would you reject the results of biblical theology?

I suspect the perceived problem depends on the dual assumption that the biblical understanding of God is supposed to be revelation, and revelation is supposed to have been given in big leaps rather than little steps. By contrast, this view assumes that science comes in many diligent little steps rather than in leaps that may suggest revelation. But alas, this is a flawed description of both science and theology. So far as science goes, it is full of big leaps of revelatory insights—what scientists have often called *Eureka!* moments. For instance, think of that moment when Michael Faraday discovered the circular flow of electromagnetism based on his belief in the mystical significance of the circle (a belief drawn from his Sandemanian religious sect by the way). And as for the theology end, the theologian makes at least as many little steps as big leaps, including the countless modest steps in which the biblical writers from Abram to Isaiah moved the Hebrews from the chaotic welter of ancient polytheism to the austere grandeur of one Creator, Yahweh. Eureka indeed.

▶ John's Rebuttal

I have a book called *Discarded Science*, by John Grant. From cold fusion to ether, it's a fascinating read. Sure, science has made mistakes. It's from these mistakes that scientists learn through a process Karl Popper described as putting forth a conjecture (or hypothesis) and then seeing if it can be refuted. Once refuted, another conjecture is made to be refuted, and so on. This is how science progresses—through a series of conjectures and refutations.

But it is delusional to equate this process with theology, in which each generation reinterprets what the Bible says because of the advancement of learning. The facts are in: religions evolve. This evolution takes place in every religion and in every society, not just in Christian ones. They evolve through the advancement of learning, especially with science. This is exactly what we would expect to find if religions were man-made. When a reasonable person looks at this development, it becomes obvious. What Randal describes as a progressive revelation is nothing more than the evolution of religion. Otherwise Randal must tell us why his God revealed himself in ways that are indistinguishable from not revealing himself at all. I don't think he can.

▶ Randal's Rebuttal

John seems to have a habit of making sweeping statements about what "biblical scholars" say. Unfortunately, many of those statements gloss a great diversity in the field of biblical studies. But let's grant John's reconstruction for the sake of argument and focus on his conclusion: "What we see here is no different than what we find in other cultures connected through the trade route of the Fertile Crescent."

There is *some* truth here, for the religion of the Hebrews is in part an organic development of its time and place, and thus it reflects the worldview of the ancient Near East (ANE). But why is that a problem? A missionary entering a new region wisely indigenizes the gospel to the culture of the people. Why would we expect less of God? Perhaps John thinks Yahweh should have provided some kind of additional evidence to establish definitively that other ANE gods like Baal are false. Fair enough. But don't we have that? While Baal has no followers today, Yahweh has over *two billion*. Isn't that some kind of evidence? But, John adds, had Baal religion survived, it too would have become monotheistic. Yeah right, and had Oldsmobile survived, it would have become the next BMW.

▶ John's Closing Statement

Why should we expect less of God? Because he could have revealed the truth about himself from the get go. This is one reason why I am a nonbeliever, because he revealed himself in ways that are indistinguishable from the surrounding ancient cultures. I need more than that to believe.

▶ Randal's Closing Statement

Both scientists and theologians falsify premises within their modes of enquiry. And both scientific and theological theories evolve over time as new data emerges. It is only a dogmatic scientism that can exclude in principle the latter from being a knowledge discourse.

◄ 3 ►

If There Is No God,
Then Everything Is Permitted

Arguing the Affirmative: **RANDAL THE CHRISTIAN**

Arguing the Negative: **JOHN THE ATHEIST**

► Randal's Opening Statement

The rain is falling steadily outside. As he steeps his cup of tea, he reflects aloud: "It has been a good career, but perhaps it is time to retire. After all, being a serial killer is hard work, especially when you've still got a day job." With a sigh he then smiles, "At least I've got much to show for all my efforts." Indeed, keepsakes from his various crimes litter his cramped home: panties in the bedroom closet with dark stains from blood spilled years ago, a collection of lipsticks buried in the bathroom medicine cabinet, and a few body parts stashed deep in a basement freezer. And he values all these trophies like the retiring company man values the Rolex watch given for thirty years of faithful service. There is no denying it. He has found this to be a fiercely satisfying life, one rich with untold pleasures as he has strived with singular purpose to fulfill every one of his endlessly dark, unspeakable desires.

He knows that others value more mundane pursuits like friendship, love, and charity. "And that's *fine* for them," he muses. "I certainly don't begrudge them their suburban sentimentalities." But he has always found pleasure and purpose in other things: being alone, preparing for the hunt, catching the victim, stuffing a wet cloth in the mouth, binding wrists . . . and everything that comes after. He looks out the window and a cruel smile spreads across his face as he recalls every desperate tear, every anguished plea.

He turns to the wall where a yellowed newspaper clipping hangs. "Police Commissioner Calls Cannibal Killer Pure Evil" the headline reads. "*Evil?*" he mutters to himself indignantly. "I guess it depends on who you ask." With that he looks intently at the picture of a somber police commissioner staring back at him from the clipping, and suddenly his countenance darkens. "Who decided that *I* am evil?" he retorts angrily. "We *all* choose our values. You choose to help others," he says to the visage accusingly, "and I choose to harm them." He suddenly waves his hand dramatically. "Some people value the human species. Others value spotted owls or sea turtles. As for me, I happen to value my own personal fulfillment. My impulses are the engine in my car, the sails on my ship. They are *my* ethical set of values. Like a preference of one's flavor of ice cream, we just disagree. You may like chocolate, but I happen to *love* vanilla."

With that his expression softens as he turns back to the dripping windowpane. It surely is all about preference, isn't it? Some people love warm sunny days, but as the rain tapers off slightly he reflects on how *he* always preferred the dark, moist chill of November evenings. He sits back in his favorite wing chair and opens his most cherished book of poetry. Though many find Frost to be overly sentimental, he loves those immortal lines for they tell his story. And so he reads aloud:

Two roads diverged in a wood, and I—
I took the one less traveled by,
And that has made all the difference.[1]

"All the difference indeed," he says wistfully. "We each choose our paths to live. And I *lived well*." As he sips his tea, he grimaces from the pain in his aging, arthritic hands. "But even so," he sighs, "I am getting older, and it probably is time to retire."

Suddenly a faint groan escapes from the basement. In a moment his expression shifts from placid contentment to blackened rage. As he leaps out of the chair he growls, "Tomorrow. I'll retire tomorrow." With that he spins on his heel, walks out of the room, and disappears down the cellar stairs.

▶ John's Opening Statement

Christians love to quote Randal's title to this chapter as a capsule description of atheist existentialists of the past like Friedrich Nietzsche, Jean Paul-Sartre, and Albert Camus. But atheists are gaining a better understanding of morality. How long will Christians keep claiming this about us? Will they do so fifty years or one hundred years from now? What if I returned the favor and said Christians still think there is divine justification for the Crusades, the Inquisition, witch hunts, Manifest Destiny, and slavery? Is that fair?

Christians use this canard so often it's nauseating. It seems self-evident to them, that is until they come to disbelieve. Then they will see things differently. The claim of Randal's in this chapter presupposes that a supernatural being is doing the permitting. But which one? There are other conceptions of gods with their own moralities. And how does this being communicate to us what is permitted? Isn't it evident that the Christian God has not effectively done so, given the biblical record and the history of the church?

There is no evidence that a Christian God is needed for morality since many non-Christian cultures have done very well for

31

themselves in their own time periods with no Christian influ-
ence at all, such as Greece during the Golden Age, the Roman
Empire, China, and Japan. This is nothing but a parochial,
narrow-minded, and uninformed claim. I think all a believer
has to do is travel the globe to see this.

There is no supernatural being out there. Therefore, the ones
doing the permitting are those of us on earth in our respective
cultures. We do not permit just anything either. In every society
we come up with moral rules just as we do when it comes to
speed limits on our highways, regulations for food preparation,
protocols for approaching different people, or criminal acts we
consider harmful to the common good. What kind of society
could we possibly have where everything is permitted anyway?
Even in a purely atheist society, rules would exist in order to
have a sane, decent, productive civilization that allows people to
live healthy, happy, and fruitful lives. It's that simple. Otherwise
societies would collapse under their own weight. And given the
fact that societies have collapsed in the past, we do learn to some
degree from our mistakes because morality evolves. Our own
societies have done the permitting, and each individual in every
society has had some say in what it permitted—even in totalitar-
ian ones. (Otherwise why have these regimes failed from within?)

A great many of our moral rules are the same ones around
the globe simply because we are all of the same human species.
That's the only objective morality we'll ever know, and it is an
objective morality even if it isn't an ultimate, absolute, or un-
changing one. Since we're rapidly becoming a world community,
we're growing closer to one global ethic. A world culture, if that
happens, will have a world ethic. This is what we'd expect from
a global community.

Morality evolves. It has done so from the very beginning.
Morality is not even unique to human beings. We find precursors of it in the nonhuman species.

But maybe I've missed the point?

If this is supposed to be an argument for the existence of
God, not even Richard Swinburne, one of the greatest living

Christian apologists, thinks it works: "I cannot see any force in an argument to the existence of God from the existence of morality."[2] If it doesn't convince him, why should it convince me, or anyone else for that matter?

The bottom line is that when it comes to morality there are problems knowing what it is (eating habits? dress codes?), how it is justified (which ethical theories?), and what motivates us to be moral (long-term rational self-interest can work just fine).

Christians have these same problems. The *Euthyphro* dilemma in Plato's dialogues shows us that positing a God as the source of morality is no answer. Does God create morality? If so, he can create any kind of morality at all. Then any acts—even horrific ones—could be morally obligatory simply because God commands them. Or must God instead derive morality from a higher source? If so, even God must obey it. Christian philosophers have all but abandoned the *divine command theory*, or at least modified it. All they can say is that God is what he is and that he does what he does. That's it.

▶ Randal's Rebuttal

John observes that "there is no evidence that a Christian God is needed for morality." But the argument is not that one needs a Christian conception of God to have morality. Rather, the argument is that we need a transcendent ground of meaning and purpose, or we are awash in a bracing moral relativism in which no view of the moral life is objectively right or wrong, good or evil.

Interestingly, John's own comments confirm this worry for he writes, "In every society we come up with the moral rules just as we do when it comes to speed limits on our highways [or] regulations for food preparation." So our moral principles are selected with the same arbitrariness as highway speed limits or modes of food preparation? "Sixty miles per hour on this stretch, oh, and no gang rape or murder for the next hundred miles please." *Really? That's it?* John may not like divine command theory (though given his criticisms, I have to wonder how well he understands it), but he surely needs *some* transcendent source of moral valuation to avoid the moral relativism that even now is wrapping its tentacles around his oblivious appendages.

▶ John's Rebuttal

"Here I am Lord, your servant Andrea Yates. Speak to me. What would you have me do today? Let's see what's in your Holy Book. Hmmm, you say, 'Happy is the one who seizes your infants and dashes them against the rocks.' Really? What do you mean? You want me to kill my children? Why them? Yes, I know they are unrighteous, lacking a care for godly things. That's my fault as a mother. Why me? You want to test me just like you tested Abraham with Isaac? Are you sure? I just can't do that. You want me to drown them in the bathtub? If you insist, Lord."

This story about Yates is true. Religious examples like these are numerous. What do they prove? That there are some sick people in our world we need to catch and incarcerate and that most of them are religious nuts doing these evil deeds.

Contrary to Randal, if there is a God, everything can be permitted, for faith-based reasoning can justify any evil deed. In fact, religion is what turns otherwise good people into evil monsters because they think God told them what to do, either "audibly" or from something they read in the Bible.

▶ Randal's Closing Statement

I believe moral values are objective and rooted in the necessity of the divine nature. John believes they are rooted in our subjective whims—whatever gets you through the night, it's all right. On that point John and our retiring serial killer are in hearty agreement. Spot of tea anyone?

▶ John's Closing Statement

It does no good to assert there is a transcendent ground of meaning unless Randal can state what it is or what morals can be derived from it. Leaving his mischaracterizations aside, morality evolves. That's what we know. That's what we see in the Bible and the church too.

◄ 4 ►

The Biblical God
Required Child Sacrifices
for His Pleasure

Arguing the Affirmative: **JOHN THE ATHEIST**

Arguing the Negative: **RANDAL THE CHRISTIAN**

► John's Opening Statement

Child sacrifice was commanded of the Israelites by Yahweh, the biblical God. In Exodus 22:29–30 we read:

> You shall not delay to offer from the fulness of your harvest and from the outflow of your presses. The first-born of your sons you shall give to me. You shall do likewise with your oxen and with your sheep: seven days it shall be with its dam; on the eighth day you shall give it to me. (RSV)

The context of this passage concerns offerings and sacrifices, and it says God requires firstborn sons to be literally sacrificed to him. Later on we find Yahweh admitting he commanded this in Ezekiel 20:25–26, where he purportedly said:

> Moreover I gave them statutes that were not good and ordinances by which they could not have life; and I defiled them through their very gifts in making them offer by fire all their first-born, that I might horrify them; I did it that they might know that I am the LORD [Yahweh]. (RSV)

Ezekiel in his time had come to realize that child sacrifice was repugnant, so this was all he could come up with to condemn it. Just deny Yahweh commanded it. Say instead that he did so because of their hardened hearts. But the logic he employed to defend the indefensible is extremely strange, for in order to punish the Hebrew parents, Yahweh demanded that they kill their children (i.e., sacrifice). How does that make any sense, especially in light of the fact that we're told Yahweh doesn't punish sons for the sins of their parents (Deut. 24:16)?

Many people in the Old Testament understood Yahweh's demands and acted accordingly. Abraham was not morally repulsed by the command to sacrifice his son Isaac, and there is no command against such a practice by Yahweh afterward (Genesis 22). Then there is Jepthah, who sacrificed his daughter (Judg. 11:29–40); David (2 Sam. 21:7–9); Ahab (1 Kings 16:33–34); Ahaz (2 Kings 16:2–3); Hoshea (2 Kings 17:17); and Manasseh (2 Kings 21:6; 2 Chron. 33:6). It was a problem for King Josiah's reforms (2 King 23:10), for Jeremiah (Jer. 7:30–31; 19:3–5; 32:35), and Ezekiel (Ezek. 16:20–21; 20:25–26, 30–31). The prophet Micah ponders if he should sacrifice his oldest son as a sin offering (Mic. 6:6–8).

The case of Micah 6:6–8 is an interesting one. In it child sacrifice is considered the greatest and highest form of sacrifice, for the prophet has a progression of three parts in pondering what will please Yahweh the most. Micah first considers sacrificing one-year-old calves; then he considers sacrificing thousands of rams; then he culminates in considering the highest offering he could give Yahweh: his firstborn son. His logic depends on child sacrifice being the greatest sacrifice of all—more than that of sacrificing the calves or rams—for the shocking conclusion of his ruminations is that even this greatest sacrifice is unacceptable to Yahweh without justice. For while all of these acts were required by Yahweh, they meant nothing without also doing acts of justice.

Child sacrifice was only later considered evil after Josiah's reforms and even more so after the Babylonian exile. Even the later rhetoric in Deuteronomy 12:29–31 and Jeremiah 7:31, 19:5, and 32:35 which condemns the practice all assumes that people thought it was acceptable to Yahweh. Otherwise why would these later authors find a need to condemn it? In other texts the practice was condemned primarily because it was offered to other deities (2 Kings 17:17; 23:10; 2 Chron. 28:3; 33:4–10; Ps. 106:38; Isa. 57:5–6; Ezek. 16:20–21; 20:26, 31; 23:37, 39). Child sacrifice to foreign gods was so prevalent that it is named as one of the reasons Yahweh sent the Assyrians to conquer Israel (2 Kings 17:16–18) and later sent the Babylonians to conquer Judah and forcibly take her people as captives (2 Kings 21:1–16; 24:1–4).

So despite some biblical exhortations that child sacrifice was alien to the worship of Yahweh, a closer inspection shows instead that this practice was within the mainstream theology of the Yahweh cult. Only at a late stage in the history of Israelite religion was child sacrifice branded as counter to the will of Yahweh.

Nearly all ancient cultures sacrificed human beings— especially virgins and children—to their gods to please them. This is utterly barbaric, conceived by a barbaric people who had no clue what an eternally good God could ever want them to do. In the New Testament Christians even interpreted the death of Jesus as God sacrificing his only begotten Son to atone for our sins.

But if Yahweh was believed to accept child sacrifice, then why should I accept anything these ancient superstitious people wrote? I can't.

▶ Randal's Opening Statement

The question here isn't whether God exists but rather whether Yahweh, the God of the Bible, has engaged in behaviors, or approved others doing so, that exclude him from being the one true God. Now at first blush some Christians will wonder how anyone could think of associating the sacrifice of children with the God of the Bible. After all, the Bible repudiates the practice in texts like Leviticus 18:21 and Ezekiel 23:37. True enough. But there are other texts that complicate matters. For instance, consider 1 Samuel 15:3: "Now go, attack the Amalekites and totally destroy all that belongs to them. Do not spare them; put to death men and women, children and infants, cattle and sheep, camels and donkeys." This text describes the intentional killing of healthy children and infants; but it actually describes more than that. The Hebrew word translated with the phrase "totally destroy" is *herem*, and it refers to anything set aside to be completely destroyed for God. To put it bluntly, to commit something to the *herem* is tantamount to *sacrificing* it to God. Thus to subject an infant to the *herem* is to sacrifice that infant to God.

This presents Christians with a trilemma. We must ask ourselves which of the following three propositions we will reject.

1. Yahweh is God.
2. The devotional killing of infants and children is always wrong.
3. The biblical passages in which Yahweh approves the devotional killing of infants and children are correctly interpreted and inerrant.

Not all of these propositions can be affirmed as true. For instance, if we assume that God would never command people

40

to perform actions that are wrong, it follows that if Yahweh is God and the devotional killing of infants and children is always wrong, then he would never command the devotional killing of infants and children. And yet we have to deal with the Bible's apparent testimony that God commanded Saul to submit infant Amalekites to the *herem*. Something, as they say, has got to give.

Obviously no Christian can reject proposition 1. (I'll leave that option to my atheist interlocutor.) But many Christians respond to this trilemma by rejecting proposition 2. They insist that God is sovereign and has rights over creation and so is within his rights to demand the devotional killing of children. While I understand why these Christians take that position, it seems to me to be a mistaken assessment of priorities. I think we have very strong intuitions that engaging in acts of devotionally killing children is always wrong, and that means that we ought to continue to accept proposition 2. The strength of our intuitions on these matters can be illuminated by reflecting on a concrete scenario.

With that in mind, consider the tragic case of Dena Schlosser of Plano, Texas. In November 2004 she amputated the arms of her infant daughter Maggie based on the perceived command of God. Most people (including most Christians) assume that God did not and indeed *could not* command such a heinous action. I agree. I am convinced that God could not have commanded a loving mother to perform such an evil action. Needless to say, I am more convinced of that than I am convinced that 1 Samuel 15:3 correctly narrates what God in fact commanded of Saul.

So I don't give up my commitment to the claim that Yahweh is God. Nor do I surrender my intuition that the devotional killing of children, be they American or Amalekite, is always evil. But I do reject the straight and inerrant reading of passages like 1 Samuel 15:3.

Admittedly this leaves me with a bit of a puzzle. If God is ultimately the primary author of Scripture, then why did he include in his revealed text passages that incorrectly depict him as demanding *herem* killings? That's a great question. But the general dilemma is hardly unique to the Bible since interpretive controversies swirl around the classic texts of all great authors. Why did the author include this statement, that situation, this character, that ending? Let us simply note that when the author is very capable and the text is widely recognized as a classic, the wiser course for the reader is to keep wrestling with the puzzling section rather than rejecting its place in the text. Given that God is a maximally competent author and the Bible the supreme classic, such a course would certainly seem advisable here.

▶ John's Rebuttal

Randal is rejecting the Bible in favor of his own moral intuitions here—ones I share. That's what he's doing. And if he can do this once, then why not just reject it all along with me? He has the gall to proclaim, despite the evidence, that God is "a maximally competent author." But if this is true, why did his God communicate in such an incompetent manner that caused a number of children to be needlessly butchered?

Where did Randal get his moral intuitions about this in the first place? Clearly not from the Bible. If we look at history, every ancient culture sacrificed human beings to their gods. Now modern civilized people don't. What happened around the globe? Lots of things. Primarily we've learned that the gods are not leaning over a celestial balcony looking down on earth and smelling the smoke of burning flesh as it rises to them. Nor do they open the floodgates of heaven to send rain for our crops. The universe is bigger than this and the rain falls naturally. So there is no one "up there" we need to appease. And there is no reason to kill our children to make it rain either.

▶ Randal's Rebuttal

There is good evidence that at some point in their history the Hebrews believed that it was proper to relate to God through human sacrifice. But what should we think of this? Some Christians believe that they were right. These folk are of the view that at that time in history God related to people through sacrifice, and since God *is* God, that's his prerogative. Other Christians demur, arguing that while the Hebrews *thought* this was the right way to relate to God, they were nonetheless wrong: God accommodated to their understanding but has since moved us beyond it. It is important to recognize that this is an intramural debate among Christians. My real interest is focused on John's fierce moral indignation toward human sacrifice; indeed, he calls it "utterly barbaric." Now what is that supposed to mean? An orchestral conductor calls his son's heavy metal music "utterly barbaric," but who's to say this isn't just a matter of taste? And if, as John believes, life has no objective purpose or value, then why isn't his indignation over human sacrifice merely another matter of taste?

▶ John's Closing Statement

What good reason is there for God to accommodate people who thought children should be butchered in his name? Can't he say "no, don't do that," like any good parent? This is a lame excuse for a God. This practice is barbaric by Randal's own standards, which is the point.

▶ Randal's Closing Statement

The apostle Paul recognized that people's moral intuitions are "written on their hearts" (Rom. 2:15). In other words, we know them innately. Consequently, they provide helpful guides for reading Scripture rightly. But for John, moral intuitions are simply subjective preferences: I like chocolate, you like vanilla; I like nurturing children, you like sacrificing them.

◄ 5 ►

Science Is No Substitute
for Religion

Arguing the Affirmative: **RANDAL THE CHRISTIAN**

Arguing the Negative: **JOHN THE ATHEIST**

► Randal's Opening Statement

In his book *Consilience*, respected scientist, well-known authority on ants, and father of sociobiology E. O. Wilson wrote that "preferring a search for objective reality over revelation is another way of satisfying religious hunger."[1] Wilson is hardly alone in the view that scientific endeavors can double as sources of religious meaning. Consider Chet Raymo, who in his book *Skeptics and True Believers* comes off at some points sounding less like a respected science writer for the *Boston Globe* and more like the latest New Age guru:

Let your soul go free for a moment into that scene outside your window, into the vistas of cosmic space and time revealed by your physics, and there encounter, gape-jawed and silent, the God of birds and birth defects, trees and cancer, quarks and galaxies, earthquakes and supernovas—awesome, edifying, dreadful and good, more beautiful and more terrible than is strictly necessary. *Let it strike you dumb with worship and fear*, beyond words, beyond logic. What is it? It is everything that is.[2]

Did you get that? There *is* a God according to Raymo, and apparently that God is . . . *the universe*. In case you were wondering, Raymo is not a pantheist—at least not of a traditional sort. Rather, he seems to be so intent on re-enchanting the de-godded universe as a means to satisfy that deep existential, religious hunger that he speaks without a blush of *worshiping* creation. Elsewhere in the book he adds:

A universe of 50 billion galaxies blowing like snowflakes in a cosmic storm is astonishing, but even more astonishing are those few pounds of meat—our brains—that are able to construct such a universe of faint light and hold it before the mind's eye, live in it, revel in it, *praise it*, wonder what it means.[3]

The superlatives just keep piling up, but what should we make of them? I think it's time for a gander at the dictionary to take a closer look at one of these religiously loaded terms. So let's consider *praise*. This verb has two basic definitions:

1. to express approval or affirmation;
2. to offer grateful homage to a deity.

Now when Raymo says we should praise the universe, I don't think he intends the milquetoast first meaning as in, "Mummy praised young Billy for using the potty." On the contrary, Raymo's invocation of praise more closely approximates the second religious meaning: he believes we're on sacred ground. With that in mind, note the striking comparison between the following two propositions:

As Chet gazed at the icon of the cross, he fell to his knees and praised Jesus.

As Deiter gazed at the images of the Hubble Deep Field, he fell to his knees and praised the universe.

This raises all sorts of questions: What sort of liturgy should one use when praising the universe? Should one read Lucretius? Henry David Thoreau? Perhaps Stephen Jay Gould (with a dollop of Chet Raymo)? And what is the appropriate temple of worship? A virgin rain forest? Maybe the site of the Mauna Loa Observatory? Finally, do we still have to tithe?

Carl Sagan offers yet another possible outlet for the sophisticated secularist in search of some old-time religion: aliens. Yes, you heard me right. When Sagan passed away in 1996, his name had already been associated for years with SETI, the search for extraterrestrial intelligence. Sagan put much effort, and much hope, into looking for alien intelligence in the universe. And more than a few commentators have observed that this search functioned for Sagan like a quasi-religious quest. Sagan hoped that we could one day establish contact with creatures of a high moral character and super intelligence:

To me, such a discovery would be thrilling. It would change everything. We would be hearing from other beings, independently evolved over millions of years, viewing the Universe perhaps very differently, probably much smarter, certainly not human.[4]

Sagan hoped not only that these super intelligent aliens could increase the speed of our computers and the fuel efficiency of our cars but that they "might play a role in unifying our squabbling and divided planet."[5] Hmm—a means to resolve all those interminable human conflicts and perhaps introduce an age of world peace? It kind of looks like salvation, doesn't it?

Satisfying religious hunger? Responding with worship and praise? Bringing a divided human race together to sing "Kumbaya"? When considering these secular versions of spirituality, I cannot help but recall the old saying that the person who ceases to worship God does not worship *nothing* but rather is liable to worship *anything*. When you attempt to shut down the impulse to worship the Creator, you end up looking for another suitably praiseworthy entity. And so we see a litany of new objects offered for worship and devotion: the scientific method, the entire universe, or perhaps even Marvin the Martian from the old Warner Brothers cartoons. And to think that some people call the doctrine of the Trinity strange.

▶ John's Opening Statement

The point of this assertion is that if we don't worship God we'll find something else to worship and that science is the god of atheists. In addition, the claim is that religion has something to offer that science cannot deliver.

Worship is an act of religious devotion directed to one or more deities involving prayer, praise, and obedience. Worship involves faith. Science involves doubt, not faith, based on sufficient evidence and the principle of methodological naturalism, which assumes every effect has a natural cause. This is a method that keeps it from being sectarian (i.e., there is no separate science for the various religions), and it continually delivers the goods.

Science has a method for arriving at the truths that religion has failed to give us. It is self-corrective as scientists try to replicate the same experiments and test various hypotheses. Its hallmark is doubt, and it focuses on that which is detectable, for we cannot detect the undetectable. Science hasn't solved everything yet, and it may never solve it all. But it has solved a lot and has much more promise of solving more.

While philosophers debate the minutiae of what makes for science, science continues to advance our knowledge of the world.

- Astronomers learned the universe is about 13.7 billion years old and it is immensely vast.
- Geologists learned the earth is just over four billion years old.
- Evolutionary biologists learned that all living organisms come from a common ancestor.
- Biomedical scientists, with their acquired knowledge of our body's hormonal, digestive, muscular, nervous, reproductive, respiratory, skeletal, immune, and circulatory systems have learned how to heal us.
- Physicists have discovered how energy is conserved as it transforms itself in a causal nexus of events.
- Chemists have discovered the composition, structure, and properties of matter down to the atomic level.
- Meteorologists have discovered the complex motions of atmosphere and how the atmosphere interacts with winds, clouds, temperature, and precipitation.
- Archaeologists have shown us that Homo sapiens originated in Africa about 200,000 years ago, reaching full behavioral modernity around 50,000 years ago.
- Neurologists have learned how our brain functions and with it much about the human psyche.

There are debates within each of these scientific disciplines, of course, but inside them are bedrock ideas the practitioners all agree about. Where is the agreement among religionists?

When it comes specifically to the Bible, archaeologists have shown us there was no worldwide flood as told in the tale of Noah and his ark. They have shown there was no exodus by the Israelites from Egypt, that the reign of King David was not as extensive as recorded in the Bible, and that there was no worldwide census at the time when Jesus was born. Philologists and historians have shown us that Moses did not pen the first five books of the Bible, that Daniel is a book filled with postdated prophecies about events that had already happened, that the Gospels were not written by contemporaries of Jesus, that the Pastoral Epistles were not written by the apostle Paul, and so on.

Science answers questions and solves problems. Religion has never answered one single question or solved one single problem. The Christian God didn't even tell us what causes lead poisoning or that drinking polluted water could kill us. He never told us which creatures would kill us if we got bitten by them or how to discover penicillin or a vaccine for tuberculosis or polio. We had to discover these things ourselves, and in the process people—mostly children—had to die before we learned about them on our own, thank you very much.

If anything, religion has always been against creative science by stalling it with censure and threats of violence.

Scientists do not worship science. They continue to check and recheck their conclusions—and their results produce wonderment. Carl Sagan, for instance, stood in awe at what science has produced. Looking at the results of astronomy in the universe evokes wonder, much like looking at an incredible piece of artwork or listening to a wonderful song. The universe is amazing to behold from the stars above to the deep oceans below. But truly seeing this for what it is comes from scientific discovery, not religion.

There is no worshiping science; we just trust its results. It has continued to produce the goods. I cannot trust religion to produce anything comparable by far. Why bet on religion? It's a bet against the overwhelming odds. It's a bet against reason itself.

▶ **Randal's Rebuttal**

I once heard of a woman who was so enamored with her Harley Davidson that she decided to marry it. Unfortunately, while a motorcycle provides a great mode of transportation, it was never intended to serve as a marital partner. I think of that as I consider secularists who have become so enamored with science that they have elevated it to be the source of transcendent meaning and purpose. While science provides a great mode of enquiry into the natural world, it was never intended to provide transcendent meaning and purpose.

Of course, John doesn't think these secularists are worshiping science or the natural world because he defines worship as "an act of religious devotion *directed to one or more deities.*" But worship doesn't require a deity. Worship is simply honor or deference paid to anything one regards as sacred, worthy of veneration, or one's ultimate concern. As a result, while God can be the object of worship, so can the scientific method, the natural world, or even super-aliens. Needless to say, the fact that you *can* worship the universe doesn't mean you *should* any more than the willingness of a magistrate to officiate at unconventional weddings means you should ride your Harley Fat Boy down the aisle.

▶ John's Rebuttal

Our brains evolved from the lower species of animals, so we have a built-in agency detector inherited from them. Animals that survived were the ones that saw faces in the leaves and the trees of the forest. This created a lot of false alarms, but because of it they had time to escape real predators. Likewise as agency detectors, the ancients saw divine agents behind strange events in their world. They did this with thunderstorms and with the sun rising or the birth of a boy. So they began to worship what they thought were divine agents behind these phenomena, and they gave over their whole lives in obedience to these agents without question.

Science is the antidote to this, not its counterpart. The word *worship* must mean something specific, otherwise it can mean anything. Sir Isaac Newton discovered the three laws of motion. If we want to throw a ball the farthest, we must release it at exactly 45 degrees from the ground.

Do we worship Newton for his amazing discovery or for this particular result? No, just as I do not worship my mother even though I love and trust her implicitly.

▶ **Randal's Closing Statement**

Does John disagree with Wilson and Raymo's panegyrics to science and the natural world? Does he eschew Sagan's existential longing for little green men? He doesn't say. John is right; worship is directed to something specific. And Wilson, Raymo, and Sagan all have very specific objects to which they ascribe maximal worth-ship.

▶ **John's Closing Statement**

Randal is playing a meaningless language game over the word *worship*, but it changes nothing. We don't build cathedrals for people to congregate for prayer to long-dead scientists, nor are their words authoritative unless we can verify them. Nor do we do this for the universe science has discovered.

◄ 6 ►

The Biblical God
Commanded Genocide

Arguing the Affirmative: **JOHN THE ATHEIST**

Arguing the Negative: **RANDAL THE CHRISTIAN**

► John's Opening Statement

There are several genocidal texts from the lips of Yahweh, the biblical God. You see it reflected in Joshua 6:16–25; Deuteronomy 2:4–34; 7:1–6; and Numbers 31:7–18 (cf. Isa. 13:13–22; Ps. 137:7–9). In Deuteronomy 20:16–18 we read:

> But as for the towns of these peoples that the LORD [Yahweh] your God is giving you as an inheritance, you must not let anything that breathes remain alive. You shall annihilate them—the Hittites and the Amorites, the Canaanites and the Perizzites, the Hivites and the Jebusites—just as the LORD [Yahweh] your God has commanded, so that they may not

teach you to do all the abhorrent things that they do for their gods, and you thus sin against the LORD [Yahweh] your God. (NRSV)

In 1 Samuel 15:1–3 we read:

> And Samuel said to Saul, "The LORD [Yahweh] sent me to anoint you king over his people Israel; now therefore hearken to the words of the LORD [Yahweh]. Thus says the LORD of hosts [Yahweh of Armies], 'I will punish what Amalek did to Israel in opposing them on the way, when they came up out of Egypt. Now go and smite Amalek, and utterly destroy all that they have; do not spare them, but kill both man and woman, infant and suckling, ox and sheep, camel and ass.'" (RSV)

The rationale for justifying genocide has fallen by the wayside among evangelicals since there can be no justifying it—not in an era that endorses the Geneva Convention, which condemns the killing of innocent noncombatants. Randal is one of these evangelicals, so I'll let him make that case for me. All such attempts fail. They ultimately force apologists to embrace a cultural relativism.

That leaves two rationales for arguing against what these texts say. First, apologists are now arguing, by virtue of conflicting texts in the Bible and the lack of archeological evidence, that these genocides never took place as stated. The texts indicate that Joshua did not accomplish the genocide of the Canaanites. Just compare Joshua 10–12, where we're told he did so, with Judges 1:21–36, where many of the Canaanites still lived in the land after Joshua died. Archaeological evidence also shows us that the geography of these texts reflects that of roughly the seventh century BC. Several of these cities did not exist at that time, or were destroyed much earlier.

Now I'm not one to argue with the evidence. In fact, there is a woeful lack of evidence for the Israelite exodus from Egypt and the Canaanite conquest. And it's well known there are discrepancies in the Bible. What the apologists are doing is using biblical discrepancies (they're all dead; they're not all dead) in their favor. They are gerrymandering these texts and thereby undermining the Bible as a divine revelation from God in order to exonerate him, and I'll leave it at that.

The second rationale apologists use is arguing that God never commanded genocide in the first place. Biblical scholars claim that what we see in these texts is a *national origin myth* used to solidify King Josiah's claims to power over other nations in the seventh century BC. It was exaggerated rhetoric, they argue. Since the later conflicting texts were probably written during Josiah's reign, Joshua becomes a type of Josiah and the narratives function as propaganda: the land is ours by divine right seen in the destruction of the inhabitants of an earlier time period.

There are problems with this argument, however. Although the archaeological evidence mentioned above is clear, it is equally clear that some cities were destroyed by the Israelites. What about this? And what can be said about Yahweh demanding the execution of women and children in Numbers 31 and 1 Samuel 15, along with the near genocide of the Benjamites in Judges 19–21? The rhetorical defense cannot exonerate Yahweh in these cases. And even if the number of noncombatants killed was exaggerated, how many women and children is Yahweh justified in having killed before it becomes immoral? Furthermore, even if these texts are rhetorical exaggerations, they have been used to justify genocides in the Crusades and the Nazi regime of the last century.

When it comes to polytheism and child sacrifice, Randal will probably defer to post-Josianic reforms that both defended monotheism and condemned child sacrifices to Yahweh. Now he has a choice to make because the texts about genocide also come from post-Josianic reforms. If Randal wants to be consistent, he cannot adopt these reforms with regard to monotheism and child sacrifice and subsequently condemn them when it comes to genocide. If he wants to maintain a progressive revelation, this heads in the wrong direction. Why would Yahweh back-track like this?

▶ **Randal's Opening Statement**

"Did you know that Jonathan Swift, author of the beloved *Gulliver's Travels*, anonymously published a tract in which he commended the mass slaughter of Irish children and the sale of their meat at market? Shocking but true! And believe it or not, he even had the gall to call it *A Modest Proposal*, as if there's anything *modest* about mass slaughter and cannibalism! It's all right there in black and white. You can read it for yourself. Swift commended genocide and cannibalism. Period."

"My friend," you reply, "I appreciate your fierce moral in-dignation, but I fear it is misdirected. Swift may have written a tract commending genocide, but that hardly means he really was commending it!"

I look at you in disbelief. "Well if he wasn't meaning to *com-mend* it, then what do you suppose he *was* meaning to do?"

"He was being *ironic*," you explain gently. "Sometimes irony is the most effective way to make one's point. It is clear that Swift wanted to challenge the callous and unjust way the En-glish aristocracy was treating the Irish peasantry, and he did so by satirizing their attitudes through a piece of radically ironic prose. This allowed Swift to challenge their assumptions more effectively than a straightforward attack on their unjust oppres-sion ever could have done."

I nod thoughtfully. "I think I see your point. So an author may state that something is the case when in fact the author does not *really* intend to state that it is the case. In fact, by affirming it he may actually be *condemning* it."

"Exactly," you nod with satisfaction. "Now you're getting it. But listen, why don't you address the Bible's commendation of genocide rather than continuing on down a rabbit trail of how Swift attacked genocide through irony?"

"Maybe it isn't a rabbit trail," I reply. "Perhaps the same point applies to the genocidal portions of the Bible."

"What?" You look at me incredulously. "Wait a minute; are you suggesting that when God said 'kill all the Canaanites' he didn't really mean it?"

"That is possible," I reply. "Think about it. How can you tell that Swift was being ironic?"

"A couple ways. First, if you know something of Swift's character you can know that he would never commend a horror like genocide. Second, you can also see his concern for justice in his other writings. But how is that relevant to the Bible's genocides?"

"Let's take your first point. One of the ways we know about God is through general revelation. Through general revelation people know that God is the most perfect and loving being there can be. Now with that in mind, it surely is very reasonable to think the most perfect and loving being would never have commanded the genocide of Jews in Nazi Germany or of Tutsis in Rwanda. But then could he really have commanded the genocide of Canaanites in ancient Palestine? I'd say that's pretty doubtful."

"So you're using reason to reject the Bible?"

"Not so. Rather, I'm using my moral intuitions as a guide for *reading* the Bible. And the fact is that *every* Christian does that. I also use the Bible itself as a guide to its own interpretation, and that brings me to my second point. If we assume the Bible is, like Swift's writings, ultimately the product of a single author, then just as we should interpret some sections of Swift's canon in light of others, so we can interpret some sections of the Bible in light of others."

"Such as . . . ?"

"Jesus's life represented a systematic deconstruction of the in-group/out-group distinctions that make genocide possible. He embraced the poor, the adulterer, the tax collector, the child, the Samaritan, and every other disenfranchised person from the out-groups of history. At the same time, he challenged the authority and status of those who were so confident that they were in the in-group, such as when he declared, 'You have heard that it was said, "Love your neighbor and hate your enemy." But I tell you, love your enemies and pray for those who persecute you, that you may be children of your Father in heaven' (Matt. 5:43–45). Jesus's whole ministry was directed against the in-group/out-group dichotomies that make evils like genocide possible. And Jesus said that if you have seen him you've seen the Father (John 14:9).

"With all that in mind, it may be that the genocidal actions are best interpreted as an ironic depiction of evil similar to Jonathan Swift's *A Modest Proposal*. Or there could be other ways that God intends the text apart from a straightforward commendation of genocide. But however I read them, in light of the God of love and mercy revealed in Jesus Christ, I cannot read them straight."

▶ **John's Rebuttal**

Randal claims it's *possible* that God was condemning genocide through irony. But his analogy breaks down because there are three significant differences between the God of the Bible and Jonathan Swift in *A Modest Proposal* that make all the difference in the world. First, Jonathan Swift was not condemning cannibalism. He was condemning the exploitation of Irish children. The full title to his book is: *A Modest Proposal for Preventing the Children of Poor People in Ireland from Being a Burden to Their Parents or Country, and for Making Them Beneficial to the Public.* Second, no one in Swift's day took cannibalism seriously. Third, no one believed Swift's words were divinely inspired, so no one ever attempted to obey what he proposed. By contrast, the God of the Bible exacerbated child exploitation with his so-called "satire" because it was written in an era when genocide was not morally questionable. Believers have likewise obeyed the Bible precisely because it's considered divinely inspired. It was obvious to everyone that Swift was writing a satire, whereas this is not the case at all with the God of the Bible. Randal's moral intuitions have merely caused him to once again reject the Bible.

▶ Randal's Rebuttal

It is not a foregone conclusion that God did, in fact, command genocide. Consider the following example.

> So Joshua subdued the whole region, including the hill country, the Negev, the western foothills and the mountain slopes, together with all their kings. *He left no survivors. He totally destroyed all who breathed*, just as the LORD . . . had commanded.
>
> Joshua 10:40 (emphasis added)

Many scholars have argued that passages like this should be interpreted hyperbolically, not unlike the sports commentator who reports, "The Yankees *killed* the Dodgers." That conclusion is reinforced by the apparent inconsistency of Deuteronomy 7:2–3 that commands the Israelites to wipe out all residents of Canaan even as it warns them not to intermarry with the Canaanites. Moreover, even if we accept that the text does narrate a genocide, that doesn't mean it is the message *for us*. For instance, Douglas Earl interprets Joshua 1–11 as an attack on the in-group/out-group contrast that makes genocide possible.[1] To this end, he points to the pivotal place of Rahab, an outsider who, contrary to the dictates of Deuteronomy 7:2, is brought within the group even as Achan, an insider, is cast out. The bottom line is that no Christian need accept that the Bible commends genocide.

▶ John's Closing Statement

In the Bible it says God commanded genocide. But since Randal insists on using biblical inconsistencies in his favor, think instead

59

about this: What modern society would accept genocide as a moral lesson unless it was, strictly speaking, on the boards? Genocide was not morally questionable in the ancient world.

▶ **Randal's Closing Statement**

A Christian need not believe God ever commanded genocide. There are different ways to read texts, and God could have appropriated human texts into his Scripture with purposes very different from the original authors. Nobody said these passages are satirical, but they need not be read straight. That's the point.

◄ 7 ►

God Is the Best Explanation
of the Whole Shebang

Arguing the Affirmative: **RANDAL THE CHRISTIAN**

Arguing the Negative: **JOHN THE ATHEIST**

► **Randal's Opening Statement**

If you spend any time listening to golden oldies radio, you've probably heard Tony Orlando's seventies hit, "Knock Three Times." The song is sung from the perspective of a lonely fellow who hears a knocking sound on the water pipes in his wall. Most of us, if we hear a knocking sound on our pipes, will probably assume that it is just produced by the changing temperature of hot water running through the pipes. But when this lonely fellow hears the knocking, he concludes that it is produced by the pretty girl living in the apartment below, presumably as some sort of flirtatious Morse code. Emboldened by this belief, the lonely fellow sings back to the girl to knock three times if she'd like him to come down and visit. Gosh, I hope for his sake that it wasn't just the hot water.

In addition to being a fine introduction to the creepy side of seventies pop music, "Knock Three Times" is also a great way to introduce two kinds of causation much discussed by philosophers:

Event causation: the process in which one event causally contributes to another event.

Agent causation: the process in which an agent undertakes to cause an event and this undertaking does cause that event.[1]

Interestingly, these definitions are sufficiently broad that *every* event can be explained as the result of one or the other. That is, it was either caused by another event or by an agent. If *we* heard those pipes knocking, we'd probably conclude that a mere *event cause* (e.g., hot water) was at play. But our lonely fellow believes that an *agent cause* (i.e., the pretty girl) created the knock as a way to say hello.

Note the reference to *undertaking* in the definition of agent causation. This signals a key difference between event and agent causes. If you attribute something to an event, then it begs the question of a prior cause for that event. For example, if you explain the knocking pipes with recourse to the hot water flow, then you require another cause to explain the hot water flow. This may lead you back to the boiler, but then you need yet another cause to explain the boiler's function, and so on. Agent causes are different since the explanation for their effects is rooted not in the prior event cause but rather in a *reason, intention,* or *desired outcome*. Thus agents can act to initiate new events without any prior determining event cause: they can *choose* to act. And in that sense they act as a *sui generis* cause.

Given the exhaustive nature of these two explanations, any particular event is the result either of a prior event or an agent. In the same way that we inquire about the cause of particular events in the universe like the knocking of pipes, so we can inquire about that truly stupendous event that happened 13.7 billion years ago when, according to the cosmologists, the universe sprang into existence out of nothing. As we seek causes to explain events in our experience, so we reasonably seek a cause to understand this grandest of all events. But which type of cause is the most plausible?

The prospects of appealing to an event cause to explain the universe's origin are bleak for the reason already noted: event causes beg the question of prior causes. As a result, if we appeal to an event then we have to explain all the events prior to that event, and this leads to an infinite regress of causes that ultimately explains nothing. In addition, it is wholly ad hoc since we have no experience of infinite causal regresses. Finally, it offers no explanation of what caused this mysterious, infinite, causal series, and thus it is really a pseudo-explanation. This dilemma recalls the father who explains to his son that the earth rests on a turtle (an event cause). Then when his son asks what the turtle rests on, the father replies that it is turtles all the way down. Even if appealing to an infinite series of event causes manages to satisfy the curiosity of a child, it is not adequate as a metaphysical explanation of the universe.

This leaves us with one remaining option: an agent cause who can simply act out of will to bring about a novel event. This is exactly the kind of causation we require to explain the universe, one that is *sui generis* and thus can avoid the fatal infinite regress. Once we recognize that the only viable causal explanation is an agent, we can inquire about its identity. Not surprisingly, when the event to be explained is the absolute origination of the material universe (the whole shebang) there *is* only one viable agent cause, and that is God.

▶ John's Opening Statement

The best answer to the existence of the whole shebang is that we do not know fully—yet. Until science helps us solve this problem, we shouldn't pretend to know. The ancient Ptolemaic model of the geocentric universe (i.e., solar system) was a complicated monster. What if people in that day simply said we don't know whether the sun or earth was the center of it all? Before Isaac Newton, what if people simply said we don't know how objects move? Before Charles Darwin, what if people simply said we don't know why the various species exist? Before the discovery of plate tectonics, what if people simply said we don't know why there are earthquakes? Before the rise of modern medicine, what if people simply said we don't know why people got sick and died? Or before the rise of the mental health profession, what if people said we don't know why people had bouts of manic depression? Why should these answers not be considered good ones? Compared to the "God did it" answer, they would have been the best answers—as we now know. The onslaught of modern science has solved so many mysteries it makes our heads spin. The God explanation has suffered so many huge hits that it's surprising anyone continues to tout it at all.

Thomas Aquinas argued that God was the unmoved mover in a series of contemporaneous events stretching hierarchically up some sort of great chain of being. But such an argument is rendered bogus in light of the concept of inertia, which does away with the need to explain motion as requiring either an infinite regress of causes or an unmoved mover. And so it goes for all of the other cosmological and design arguments to the existence of God—something I won't pursue further here.

Just look at it this way. Christians either argue from the gaps in scientific knowledge or they don't. If they do, then they are arguing from ignorance (a known, informal fallacy), contrary to the success of science as it closes previous gaps only to uncover more of them. If they don't, claiming instead that their God is merely the sustainer of creation, then God plus the universe looks indistinguishable from a universe without God at all. In either case it seems apparent that the God explanation is one we can do without as either based on ignorance or in rendering it superfluous.

As modern science advances, it creates an ever-increasing number of new mysteries that scientists are in the process of solving. So faith will probably always find a foothold in mystery.

This is the reason why I must show Randal's faith is impossible before he will ever consider it to be improbable, which is an unreasonable standard. My point is that science, not faith, solved the mysteries of the past, and it is science, not faith, that has opened up the number of new mysteries today. Faith by contrast has no method and solves no mysteries. Like a parasite it survives only as it clings to that which has life. Faith by itself produces nothing and is dead without mysteries.

As far as I can tell, even if there is a god of some kind, he may have only created what Edward Tryon and Stephen Hawking both describe as a "quantum wave fluctuation"[2] and then committed divine suicide afterwards, or died in order to create. Or instead, a god may exist who is guiding the universe ultimately toward an evil purpose but has maliciously chosen to present himself as benevolent to trick us. If such a trickster god exists, then all of the evidence leading Christians to conclude their good God exists was simply planted there to deceive us by that very same God. I can see no reasonable objection to these other god-hypotheses once we allow them into our equations. They are just as possible as what any Christian or Muslim or Jew believes. That's why scientists cannot posit god explanations for answers to the origin of the universe, for once we allow them into our equations, most any god will do.

So even if there is a God who created the whole shebang, then as far as I can tell there is no reason to believe this god is Randal's God. Such an entity is therefore an unnecessary hypothesis. It actually gets in the way of solving the mysteries of existence, as history repeatedly shows.

▶ **Randal's Rebuttal**

John thinks we should wait for science to explain the universe's origin. He suggests, for example, that the "concept of inertia" (that is, Newton's first law of motion) does away with the need for an "unmoved mover" (that is, an agent cause). But this reflects a fundamental failure to understand the problem. The *entire universe*, including all its energy and matter—Newton's first law of motion—and even time itself sprang into existence out of nothing 13.7 billion years ago. Science can study the universe once it exists, but it can never explain what brought it into existence. To do that you reason not from a gap of ignorance but rather from the only type of cause known to be capable of producing the observed effect: an agent of great power. If that looks a lot like God, then so be it.

▶ John's Rebuttal

The only pseudo-explanation is the God explanation, as I explained. Why is this supposed agent exempt from all our experience that everything begins to exist and will cease to exist? And if he can be exempt, then why can't the universe itself be exempt? To suppose this agent is a spiritual being who was timeless before creation actually makes things worse. When did this agent ever get a chance to choose his or her own nature or learn that which he or she knows? Can we really imagine a being who never learned anything? Can we really imagine a being who cannot think, since doing so means a conclusion has not been reached yet? How did this nonmaterial agent create a material universe out of nothing unless there is some aspect that this agent shares with a material world? How did a timeless being create the universe in time, since the very decision to create it would be simultaneous with the act of creating it? The universe would therefore be an eternal one if he created it at all, and such a being would never be found timeless. Finally, why did he create anything at all, since he neither needs nor wants anything at all?

▶ Randal's Closing Statement

John never challenged the claim that all events are caused either by a prior event or an agent. Nor did he explain how the universe's absolute origin could be explained by a prior event. So our choice is clear: explain the universe via the only known type of cause (an agent) to produce the observed effect or invoke mystery and a misbegotten faith in the absolute power of science.

▶ John's Closing Statement

With Randal's God explanation there is no reason to investigate why the universe exists, since he says science can't do this. This is the standard theistic response to the unsolved mysteries of the past. Why keep betting on faith to solve them when it has solved nothing so far?

◄ 8 ►

The Biblical God
Does Not Care Much about Slaves

Arguing the Affirmative: **JOHN THE ATHEIST**

Arguing the Negative: **RANDAL THE CHRISTIAN**

► John's Opening Statement

This topic raises the issue of the goodness of the divine revelation in the Bible for a good, omnipotent, and omniscient God. It also raises the problem of suffering (or evil) if such a God exists. If any issue speaks against the goodness of the biblical conception of God, this is it.

Former American slave Frederick Douglass described how his Christian master whipped his aunt right before his young eyes:

> He took her into the kitchen, and stripped her from neck to waist. He made her get upon the stool, and he tied her hands to a hook in the joist. After rolling up his sleeves, he

commenced to lay on the heavy cowskin, and soon the warm, red blood came dripping to the floor. . . . No words, no tears, no prayers, from his gory victim, seemed to move his iron heart from its bloody purpose. The louder she screamed, the harder he whipped; and where the blood ran fastest, there he whipped longest. He would whip her to make her scream, and whip her to make her hush; and not until overcome by fatigue, would he cease to swing the blood clotted cowskin.[1]

A religion should be judged based on how it treats the defenseless. Slaves are the most defenseless of them all. Given the cruelty toward slaves that we see in the Bible and that has been acted out in history, all civilized people should reject Christianity as nothing but a religion created in a barbaric era.

The pro-slavery movement had the better arguments. They argued slavery was never condemned in the Bible but instead divinely sanctioned by the patriarchs (Gen. 9:24–27; 12:5, 16; 14:14; 16:1–9; 20:14; 24:35–36; 26:13–14; 47:15–25), incorporated into Israel's national laws (Exodus 21; Leviticus 25), and authorized by Jesus (Luke 12:35–48; 14:15–24) and the apostles (Eph. 6:5; Col. 3:22–25; 1 Tim. 6:1–6; Titus 2:9–10; Philemon; 1 Pet. 2:18–19). They denied the abolitionist claim that other passages dissolved the social distinction between master and slave (1 Cor. 12:13; Gal. 3:28; Col. 3:11) since the apostles spoke elsewhere about this relationship, even to the point of saying a person was "called" to be a slave (1 Cor. 7:20–22) or to suffer under a harsh master (1 Pet. 2:18–19). Biblical scholar Hector Avalos argues with regard to Galatians 3:28: "Paul does not mean that slaves do not exist literally anymore. Thus, 'there is no slave or free' cannot mean 'there exist no slaves or free people.' Otherwise, if slaves do not literally exist anymore, then nor do free people."[2] Only abuses were discouraged (Col. 4:1), although the Bible did not regard beating a slave nearly to death as abusive (Exod. 21:20–21).

Some apologists claim the word for slaves in the Old Testament (*'ebed*) does not connote ownership of the person. But Avalos argues such a conclusion "is clearly contradicted" by

Leviticus 25, "for it uses the word *'ebed* when describing how the Israelites are allowed to buy slaves. Verse 45 states that an *'ebed* 'may be your property' and may be inherited by the slave-master's children (v. 46)." Avalos asks, "If buying and inheriting an *'ebed* does not 'connote ownership of a person,' then what does?"[3] Contrary to apologists who claim the abolition movement was inspired by the Bible, Avalos argues convincingly that "the Bible's stance on slavery posed an enormous, and sometimes insuperable, challenge for abolitionists."[4]

To say evil men distorted the Bible for their own greedy purposes defies the facts. To say we would think otherwise if we were Caucasian born and raised in the Antebellum South defies the facts. To say God could not have unequivocally condemned slavery in the Bible defies the facts.

Nonetheless, why would a good God give human beings the freedom that we have so badly abused? A two-year-old child should not be given a razor blade. If we give him or her one, then we will be blamed if that child hurts himself or herself or others with it. The giver of a gift is to be blamed when he or she gives something to a person knowing in advance that the person will abuse the gift. Likewise, if God gave us the freedom to enslave others, he is to be blamed for what we do with that gift. God could have created us all with one color of skin so there would be no race-based slavery. He could have implanted in us an inviolable moral code against enslaving others, or made us suffer from severe nausea at the very thought of it. But he didn't.

▶ Randal's Opening Statement

On October 28, 1787, young politician William Wilberforce wrote in his journal: "God Almighty has set before me two great objects, the suppression of the slave trade and the reformation of manners [or morals]." Based on this call, Wilberforce spent the rest of his life as a member of Parliament in Britain, working first for the abolition of the slave trade (achieved in 1807) and then of slavery itself (achieved in 1833), driven by the conviction that God desires to liberate all peoples.

But wait a minute. Wasn't Wilberforce aware that God *doesn't* really care about slaves? After all, God approved of the institution of slavery in ancient Israel. And the apostle Paul directed the escaped slave Onesimus to return to his slave boss (Philem. 1:12).

In his *A Letter on the Abolition of the Slave Trade*, Wilberforce addresses the role of slavery in the Bible. To begin with, he notes that the belief that God made a concession to slavery in ancient Israel doesn't oblige one to accept the morality of the institution today. (By analogy, conceding that a developing economy may require protectionist trade policies doesn't allow us to conclude similar policies are defensible for a developed economy.) Moreover, he points out that God advised the merciful treatment of slaves and stipulated that they should be emancipated after a fixed period of time.[5] Finally, Wilberforce pointed out that we are now in a radically different situation since Christ "has done away with all distinctions of nations, and made mankind all one great family, all our fellow creatures are now our brethren."[6] Indeed this theme is reflected in the two Bible passages that adorn the title page of his book:

> There is neither Greek nor Jew, circumcision nor uncircumcision, Barbarian, Scythian, bond nor free: but Christ is all, and in all. Put on therefore . . . bowels of mercies, kindness.
>
> Colossians 3:11–12 KJV

> And [God] hath made of one blood all nations of men for to dwell on all the face of the earth.
>
> Acts 17:26 KJV

We can summarize Wilberforce's views as follows: When God entered into history, he accommodated himself to the flawed social institutions of the time. But as he did so, he began to renovate those institutions from the inside out with the end goal being the liberation of all peoples. This brings us to Paul's decision to send escaped slave Onesimus back to Philemon. Yes, he sends him back, but at the same time he appeals to the master to welcome the slave as he would welcome Paul himself (Philem. 1:17). Paul knew that no institution of slavery can be sustained once one truly grasps the gospel of grace and accepts the full equality of the oppressed class. In other words, the letter we call "Philemon" is not a concession to slavery but a Trojan horse into its heart.

While there is much to commend Wilberforce's redemptive view of history, some Christians will remain reluctant to accept the notion that God ever accommodated himself to slavery. For these people there is another more radical possibility. Perhaps the ancient Israelites were simply *mistaken* to believe that God had consented to the institution of slavery. Maybe they forgot the lessons of the liberation from slavery in Egypt as they immediately fell into the pattern of enslaving others while rationalizing their behavior by projecting their actions onto the will of the Almighty. And maybe God allowed this errant reading of his will to be included within his book precisely as a sober warning to the rest of us—a demonstration of how quickly we also move from liberation to the oppression of others. (Think, for example, of the parable of the unmerciful servant in Matthew 18:21–35.) In this view the tension with the oppression of other peoples hinted at in prophets like Ezekiel emerges fully with the life, teachings, and sacrificial death of Christ.

While these two views diverge sharply on their assessment of slavery in ancient Israel, they agree that God sent Christ to establish a kingdom of mercy and justice for all people in which "there is neither Jew nor Gentile, neither slave nor free, nor is there male and female, for you are all one in Christ Jesus" (Gal. 3:28). Whatever one thinks of slavery in ancient Israel, this theme of the blessing of all nations is consistent in Scripture from the calling of Abraham (Gen. 18:18) to the culmination of the New Jerusalem (Rev. 21:26). And it is this theme and hope that has inspired Christian reformers from William Wilberforce in the eighteenth century to the International Justice Mission in the twenty-first. For that reason, Christians everywhere work for that day so beautifully described by Dr. Martin Luther King Jr.:

When all of God's children—, black men and white men, Jews and Gentiles, Protestants and Catholics—will be able to join hands and sing in the words of the old Negro spiritual: "Free at last! Free at last! Thank God Almighty, we are free at last!"[7]

▶ John's Rebuttal

The information given on Wilberforce is sorely outdated. He discouraged the use of the Bible in debates about slavery, and he threw his support behind another form of slavery in Sierra Leone known as *apprenticeships*.[8] Paul in Acts 17:26 basically repeats Seneca and Cicero's sentiments, so there isn't anything there that can be credited to Christianity.[9]

I find it incredibly dense to see Christians like Wilberforce arguing that God did the best he could to abolish slavery. He could have condemned it from the beginning, consistently saying, "Thou shalt not enslave human beings or beat them into servitude." There are no circumstances where a loving God could ever think it was expedient to allow such an utterly vile institution to exist. None.

If instead the Israelites misunderstood what God was saying, then they probably got other things wrong, such as the very existence of that God. So either God did not do his best or the ancient Israelites invented their particular God from out of their own superstitious barbaric outlook, in an era when slavery was acceptable.

▶ Randal's Rebuttal

While John carefully amasses a number of alleged biblical problem texts on slavery, he all but ignores the key redemptive passages like Galatians 3:28—a text that Paul Jewett and Marguerite Shuster rightly refer to as the "Magna Carta of humanity."[10] John does deal briefly with this text by quoting Hector Avalos's observation that Paul cannot be interpreted as denying the existence of slaves. While this is true, it is also wholly irrelevant. The real lesson here is that when this text affirms the equality of all people in Christ, it definitively undermines the moral justification for slavery. While the Christian has a clear mandate to fight slavery, in what does John root *his* moral indignation? Ironically, it appears that John critiques the Christian tradition on slavery by tacitly drawing upon the moral absolutes of that very tradition.

▶ John's Closing Statement

It's irrelevant if an atheist makes this argument. The facts speak for themselves. Christians are leaving their faith because of it. So where does Randal get his own sense of moral indignation when his God does not share it? He gets it from our advancing culture and the sciences, just like I do.

▶ Randal's Closing Statement

John charges that God should have been clearer in his condemnation of slavery. I charge that John should be clearer on the objective ground that drives *his* condemnation of slavery. Reformers from William Wilberforce to Martin Luther King Jr. have been driven by the inherent equality of all people made in the image of God as they work for his peaceable kingdom. What drives John?

◄ 9 ►

If There Is No God,
Then We Don't Know Anything

Arguing the Affirmative: **RANDAL THE CHRISTIAN**

Arguing the Negative: **JOHN THE ATHEIST**

▶ Randal's Opening Statement

Over the last few hours you've been following a rough alpine hiking trail over an open rock face, guided by the intermittent rock piles that you believe were placed there by park rangers to keep you on the trail. As you arrive at the end of the trail, however, you come to believe those rock piles were not actually placed there by park rangers. On the contrary, you now believe they were placed there randomly by the happenstance processes of wind and erosion. So now you ask yourself, "If the rocks were randomly placed, what is the likelihood that they've kept me on the true trail?" You turn back and look at the vast rock face you just traversed. While following those random piles of rocks may have gotten you across the face, you have little reason to believe they also kept you on the trail. After all, for all you know there are potentially *millions* of possible paths across the face. So the likelihood that you actually followed the true path is very low.

The *backpacker's dilemma* illustrates the atheist's problem of knowledge. According to atheism, our cognitive faculties are analogous to those piles of rocks. In the same way that the rock piles were formed without any intention to mark the trail, so our cognitive faculties were formed without any intention to identify the truth. And just as there are potentially millions of ways to traverse the rock face apart from the correct one, so there are potentially millions of ways to navigate this world apart from having true beliefs about it. In the same way that our confidence that we have correctly followed the trail is lost once we come to believe the rock piles were formed apart from a super-intending truth-directed intelligence, so is our confidence that we correctly track the truth undermined once we believe something similar about our cognitive faculties.[1] Consequently, we have no reason to accept that our cognitive faculties are generally directed toward truth rather than mere adaptation. And this means we have no reason to believe we have true beliefs rather than merely adaptive ones.

An atheist may retort, "But surely true beliefs are also the most adaptive, and so natural selection would select the most effective truth-producing faculties. Since we have survived as a species, we can know that we have largely true beliefs." The problem is that there is no reason to think this is actually true. To illustrate, imagine a man walking in the forest who comes across a poisonous plant. Any belief that keeps him from eating the plant is adaptive. That includes the one true belief that "this plant is poisonous," as well as countless false ones like "this plant is sacred," "eating this plant is bad luck," and "this plant is my uncle reincarnated." Each one of these beliefs produces the adaptive behavior (refraining from eating), but only one is true.

And so to believe that our cognitive faculties happen to produce beliefs that are not only largely adaptive but also largely true is as ungrounded as thinking our ticket will win the lottery: we may *hope* this, but we can't rationally *believe* it.

Atheists who honestly face this problem are often led to some rather extreme reactions. Consider the case of philosopher Richard Rorty, whose response was to toss out the very *definition* of truth as correspondence to reality and redefine it in terms of pragmatic usefulness. In other words, a true belief is not one that keeps you on the right trail but merely one that gets you across the rock face:

> If one takes the core of pragmatism to be its attempt to replace the notion of true beliefs as representations of "the nature of things" and instead to think of them as successful rules for action, then it becomes easy to recommend an experimental, fallibilist attitude.[2]

Rorty's radical redefinition of truth illustrates nicely the internal tensions within an atheistic worldview. Even so, it really begs the question: If a person must choose between truth and atheism, why would anyone choose the latter?

▶ John's Opening Statement

This simply cannot be true given evolution as a scientific fact. There are precursors of our own reasoning abilities found in animals. There is morality, consciousness, tool-making, learning, problem-solving, community, and communication.[3] At some point human beings could comprehend that an A(pple) is an A(pple) and not an O(range), so A=A and A≠O. They also comprehended something we must all do to stay alive.

1. If we want to stay alive then we must eat.
2. We want to stay alive.
3. Therefore we must eat.

The above is a logical argument known as *modus ponens*, which is one of the most basic rules of logic. I see no reason to think we need a God to know this. All we need is an information processor that computes the steps. And we have one: a brain. Evolution explains where that came from quite nicely. If this weren't a rational universe, we wouldn't have developed the logic that arises from observing it. A different universe would produce a different kind of logic—whatever that could possibly be—and our brains would then have evolved to compute that logic instead.

The brains of dogs, donkeys, and dolphins work to help them survive. The brains of chimps, chicks, and chipmunks help them survive. The brains of pigs, porcupines, and platypuses help them survive. If their brains had not evolved as they did, then they wouldn't have survived. Why then is it different with human beings?

What Randal claims is not just that our brains are unreliable but that they are utterly and completely unreliable (apart from luck) to know the truth. That is, if naturalism is true, we should not trust them at all. I find this to be a nearly impossible argument to defend, yet *that's* the argument he has to make.

Our senses aren't *perfectly* reliable, but they are *very* reliable. Our reasoning has many flaws, but it is reliable enough for telling the difference between better methods and worse ones. Our brains are computers that evolved to run various information processing routines. These then evolved to be in our brains because they were more successful at discovering the truth than random chance. But they aren't perfectly successful. So we developed tools—new technologies—to improve the accuracy of our information processing, and those tools include language, mathematics, logic, and the scientific method. These are like software patches that we run in our brains to correct the errors to which our brains are still biologically prone. But logic, math, and scientific method aren't products of evolution. They're products of intelligent *human* design. They are analogous to eyeglasses, microscopes, or telescopes, which we invented to see better; or axes, which we invented to cleave wood better; or wheels, which we invented to move things around better. We've also built our own computers that can perform every kind of logical reasoning there is, and we've even built computers that can learn how to reason logically on their own.

Our ability to learn any system of tricks and invent tools necessary to figure out how the universe works derives from our evolved capacity to use symbolic language and from our evolved capacity to solve problems and predict behaviors through hypothesis formation and testing. These are all of inestimable value to survival. They also entail the ability to do the same things in any domain of knowledge, not just in the directly useful domains of resource acquisition, threat avoidance, and social system management.[4]

Christians have their own difficulties when justifying reason. Nominalists, following William of Ockham (1288–1348), argue that God does not have a nature, and as such, he does not have the property (or attribute) of reason. They argue that a full-blown concept of God is one in which he created reason; otherwise where did it come from? The alternative that he must obey the dictates of reason implies that reason itself is *independent* of God; and if that's the case, we don't need God to justify reason. So whence comes reason on Christian grounds?

▶ **Randal's Rebuttal**

John observes that "the brains of dogs, donkeys, and dolphins work to help them survive. The brains of chimps, chicks, and chipmunks help them survive. The brains of pigs, porcupines, and platypuses help them survive. If their brains had not evolved as they did, then they wouldn't have survived." He then asks incredulously: "Why then is it different with human beings?" It isn't, and that's exactly the problem. In John's atheism our brains evolved to *help us survive, not to find truth*. In all his comments John begs the question by *assuming* that adaptive beliefs will be largely true ones. But as I pointed out with the illustration of the rock face and the example of the poisonous plant, there are countless false beliefs that are adaptive in addition to the one true belief. Thus John's confidence in his cognitive faculties is as irrational as the belief that you have the winning ticket in the lottery. As for John's final, desperate reference to William of Ockham, that is irrelevant since I reject nominalism.

▶ **John's Rebuttal**

If a particular prehuman species saw a lethal poisonous plant and ate it, then that species died out in favor of a different species that didn't eat it (or a subset within that same species). Whole species have become extinct because they did the wrong things. As a result, 99 percent of all species that have ever existed are extinct. Evolution works this way, and it's very wasteful. But since we've survived as a species, we know we have largely acquired true beliefs because we're here! This is noncontroversial and obvious since evolution is a fact—something Randal has chosen not to debate in this book. Unfortunately, some members of the human species may conclude a poisonous plant is *sacred*. Will they survive?

How does Randal propose we know something if it isn't useful to us and discovered by trial and error? Surely he understands the difficulties with the correspondence and coherence theories of truth given that we don't have access to the *thing-in-itself*, as Immanuel Kant successfully argued. We're not talking in terms of ontology—about that which exists. Instead, we're always talking in terms of epistemology, that is, how we can know it. Pragmatism works despite the fact that Randal doesn't like the conclusion.

▶ **Randal's Closing Statement**

John first restates that we must have true beliefs because we survived, even though I already pointed out that for every true and adaptive belief there are millions of false adaptive beliefs. Next, he concedes a Kantian skepticism while desperately claiming that I am obliged to join him. Sorry John, I have no desire to join you in your epistemological hole. But when you're ready, theism provides a clean escape.

▶ John's Closing Statement

Adaptive beliefs are the ones that are useful for our survival. The rest of our beliefs, no matter how many of them we have, are either irrelevant to our survival or detrimental to it. I think religious beliefs are largely detrimental to our survival as a species in a world with weapons of mass destruction.

◄ 10 ►

The Biblical God
Does Not Care Much
about Women

Arguing the Affirmative: **JOHN THE ATHEIST**

Arguing the Negative: **RANDAL THE CHRISTIAN**

► John's Opening Statement

As I said earlier, a religion should be judged based on how it
treats the defenseless. Women have largely been defenseless in
a male-dominated society stemming in the West from what we
find in the Bible. Given the cruelty toward women that we see
there and acted out in history, all civilized people should reject
Christianity as nothing but a religion created in a barbaric, sexist
era. While there are a few positive female role models and pro-
women statements in the Bible, overall it is anti-women. These
texts need to be explained, not explained away.

A man was created first, not a woman, so Paul argued that men alone are created in the image of God (1 Cor. 11:3–9). The woman was merely created to be a man's helper (Gen. 2:18–24). Women are considered the easily deceived weaker sex who can mislead men just as Eve misled Adam (1 Cor. 11:3; 1 Pet. 3:7). That's why God said men will rule (or *domineer*) over them (Gen. 3:16). That's why Paul told women to keep silent in his churches (1 Cor. 14:34–35; see also 1 Tim. 2:11–14). That's also why women are to be subject to their husbands "in everything" (Eph. 5:24).

In fact, as biblical scholar Michael Coogan argues, "Husbands and fathers had virtually absolute control over their wives and daughters."[1] Sarah called her husband "lord" (Gen. 18:12) and "obeyed" him (1 Pet. 3:6; see vv. 1–6). These things reflect the status of a wife, writes Coogan, for "she was under her husband's rule, she was his property."[2] The woman's value as property was considered just below a man's house but above his servants, who were in turn above his oxen and donkeys, since that's the descending order of value mentioned in the tenth commandment (Exod. 20:17). Biblical scholar Drorah O'Donnell Setel informs us there were no words for *marriage*, *wife*, or *husband* in the legal texts of the Old Testament: "The terms commonly translated as such mean 'taking' in the sense of taking possession of something."[3]

Fathers could sell their daughters as slaves if they wanted to (Exod. 21:7–11). Coogan tells us that for "a woman marriage was not all that different from being sold as a slave wife" anyway, since brides were always bought with a price, some of them after being seduced (Exod. 22:16–17) or even raped (Deut. 22:28–29).[4] With divine approval, virgins could be captured as sex slaves from the spoils of war (Num. 31:17–18) or simply stolen from others (Judg. 21:10–23).

Biblical scholar Carol L. Meyers informs us that "the Bible as a whole is androcentric, or male-centered, in its subject matter, its authority, and its perspectives."[5] It was a society in which women were excluded from positions of value and authority, and the various commandments show no female concerns at all.

The really horrific stuff is how Yahweh treated his unfaithful wife, Israel. Biblical scholar Susanne Scholz informs us, "God turns out to be a rapist."[6] His wife is described as whoring after other lovers, so in return Yahweh sexually violates her and says she is to be blamed for her punishment. Biblical scholar J. Cheryl Exum translates Isaiah 3:17 like this: "The Lord will make bald the heads of the daughters of Zion, and the Lord will bare their cunts."[7] In Jeremiah 13:22–26 Yahweh announces the rape of Jerusalem, and then he does this with "the obscene practice of exposing women by drawing their legs over their heads in order to uncover their vulvas completely."[8]

Yahweh punished his unfaithful wives like this, both Samaria and Jerusalem. (Yes, Yahweh was a polygamist!) The prophets Hosea (chapter 2), Jeremiah (chapter 13), and Ezekiel (chapters 16 and 23) tell us about their punishment. Yahweh's unfaithful wives were stripped bare before a mob, mutilated, and killed. In the prophetic mind these punishments were allegories using the husband and wife relationship, of course. But they must have had a meaning for the people to whom they were spoken; otherwise it wouldn't make good sense to use them. Then comes a warning from Yahweh himself that he did this so "that all women may be instructed not to act promiscuously as you did" (Ezek. 23:48).[9] Men in that era surely used these texts to justify their own sexual punishments since Yahweh did these same kinds of things.

What a wonderful life women had in the Bible. *Not!*

▶ Randal's Opening Statement

It was June 1, 1843, when Isabella Baumfree first heard the Spirit's call on her life. Shortly thereafter she changed her name to "Sojourner Truth," became a Methodist, and began to campaign actively for abolition and women's rights. Less than a decade later Sojourner dictated her story to her friend Olive Gilbert. The resulting *Narrative of Sojourner Truth* includes this riveting description of her encounter with Jesus:

"Who *are* you?" she exclaimed, as the vision brightened into a form distinct, beaming with the beauty of holiness, and radiant with love. She then said, audibly addressing the mysterious visitant—"I *know* you, and I *don't* know you." Meaning, "You seem perfectly familiar; I feel that you not only love me, but that you always *have* loved me—yet I know you not—I cannot call you by name." When she said, "I know you," the subject of the vision remained distinct and quiet. When she said, "I don't know you," it moved restlessly about, like agitated waters. So while she repeated, without intermission, "I know you, I know you," that the vision might remain—"Who are you?" was the cry of her heart, and her whole soul was in one deep prayer that this heavenly personage might be revealed to her, and remain with her. At length, after bending both soul and body with the intensity of this desire, till breath and strength seemed failing, and she could maintain her position no longer, an answer came to her, saying distinctly, "It is Jesus." "Yes," she responded, "it is *Jesus.*"[10]

From this amazing experience, Sojourner went on to become one of the greatest activists for women's rights in history. She spoke with missionary zeal about the equality of the genders and races, guided and emboldened by the divine call upon her life.[11]

Apparently John thinks Sojourner was wrong. He thinks Jesus didn't care about women and that Sojourner didn't understand the faith she professed half as well as John does. But why think this? Is it such a surprise that Sojourner was called by the same Jesus who bucked social convention by teaching women (Luke 10:38–42) and receiving support from them (Luke 8:1–3)? Who expressed maternal care for Jerusalem as a hen gathers her chicks (Matt. 23:37; cf. Ps. 91:4)? Who, though hanging on the cross, showed concern for the well-being of his mother (John 19:26–27)? Who reserved his first post-resurrection appearance for his female disciple Mary (John 20:14–18)? Is it a surprise that she was called in the same Spirit who poured out his gifts on all people without discrimination (Acts 2:17–18)? Is it a surprise that she was called with the same church that elevated women by placing them in prominent roles in ministry (Acts 18:18, 26; 21:9; Rom. 16:7; 1 Cor. 16:19)? Is it a surprise that she was called to minister to the same two genders that share equality in the image of God (Gen. 1:27)?

In 1851 Sojourner delivered her great "Ain't I a Woman?" speech (though she did so in the Dutch accent she learned from her slave masters and not the Southern drawl of the popular imagination). The speech, as recorded by Frances Gage, begins as follows:

> Dat man over dar say dat woman needs to be helped into carriages, and lifted over ditches, and to have de best place eberywhar. Nobody eber helps me into carriages or ober mud puddles, or gives me any best place. . . . And ar'n't I a woman?[12]

There can be little doubt that Sojourner did not need the aid of any man to help her into carriages or over ditches. But she certainly did hope they would treat her, her life, her works, and her understanding of her faith with respect. It is here that one cannot help but note the sad irony in John's bold assertions. While he may respect her life's works, he wants us to believe that she didn't understand her faith and that it had no connection with those works. So ultimately we must choose. Shall we listen to John, the atheist, as he seeks to instruct the former slave in the faith she professed? Or shall we trust the former slave turned abolitionist, preacher, and women's rights activist, she whose voice rings down from history providing an indignant answer to John's provocative charges: "And ar'n't I a woman?"

▶ John's Rebuttal

Elizabeth Cady Stanton and Susan B. Anthony were the atheist leaders of the early women's rights movement. Together with Christians like Sojourner Truth they changed the world for the better *based on the moral intuitions that Randal and I share that Yahweh and the biblical writers emphatically did not share.* There is a running joke among skeptics that sometime in the future when homosexuality and animals rights are fully embraced by Christians (something already in process), they will argue that Christianity was the catalyst for these social changes, just as they now falsely argue their faith was the catalyst for the origins of science, the abolition of slavery, and women's rights. It's only a matter of time, but it's utter bunk.

Morality evolves. Period. As it does, Christians reread the Bible and look inside for the minority voices to support what they have come to accept on other grounds. They simply turn a deaf ear to the majority voices, something I call cherry-picking. Do Christians really think that a God who could threaten to kill off all the Israelites for disobedience could not have enforced a decent, civilized attitude toward women? Their delusion is probably never seen more than here.

▶ **Randal's Rebuttal**

John piles up a long list of biblical texts in an attempt to establish that Sojourner could not have been called. "These texts" he declares, "need to be explained, not explained away." They *can* be explained in two ways.

To begin with, on a closer reading many texts present no problem. Consider John's complaint that man was created first in Genesis. Does this diminish women? Well does it diminish human beings that they are created after fish and birds? On the contrary, the more significant created beings are set later in the narrative. If anything, the status of woman as final creation *elevates* her. As for the reference to the woman as man's helper (*ezer*), that isn't so bad once you realize God is also described as our helper (Ps. 33:20).

But are there other biblical texts that represent androcentric or even misogynistic perspectives? To the extent that such texts do exist, we are within our rights to read them in light of the deeper themes of equality and redemption from creation to the ministry of Jesus and the Spirit that guided Sojourner throughout her life.

▶ John's Closing Statement

Probably the main reason I have set myself against the Christian faith is because of how it denigrates women. And it is pure hubris for a nonbiblical scholar like Randal to dispute what most biblical scholars have concluded about this issue. He's sneaking his own foreign, moral intuitions into the texts.

▶ Randal's Closing Statement

John charges me with "cherry-picking" the Bible even as he ignores the most pertinent biblical texts on the image of God and the community of redemption. That's ironic, but not half as ironic as his absolutist, stentorian denunciation of patriarchy combined with his milquetoast confession that "morality evolves."

◄ 11 ►

Love Is a Many Splendored Thing, but Only if God Exists

Arguing the Affirmative: **RANDAL THE CHRISTIAN**

Arguing the Negative: **JOHN THE ATHEIST**

► Randal's Opening Statement

Andrew Brown opens his book *The Darwin Wars* with an account of the suicide of George Price. As Brown explains, Price became convinced through his work in theoretical biology that true selflessness and virtue were impossible:

> He had reformulated a set of mathematical equations that shows how altruism can prosper in a world where it seems that only selfishness is rewarded.[1]

It is not that creatures cannot act selflessly. Price recognized that they can; however,

though his equation showed that truly self-sacrificing be-
haviour can exist among animals, and even humans, it also
seemed to show that there is nothing *noble* in it. Only behavior that helps to spread the genes that cause it can survive in
the very long term.[2]

Price's discovery was too much for him to bear, and it spurred
on his emotional and mental demise. He simply could not live
in a world where love was nothing more than an aid to survival.

Over the last thirty years evolutionary psychologists have
turned their attention to the same territory once explored by
Price. And the conclusion has been that from the perspective
of evolutionary history, love is emotional attachment that has
value in virtue of being an aid to survival and reproduction. For
example, Campbell and Ellis describe the penchant for paired
bonding in human beings as follows: "Given that men have a
genetic interest in the survival of their offspring, they were able
to benefit reproductively by forming committed, investing relationships that would have reliably increased the probability of
offspring survival."[3] Love, on this view, has its biological value
in ensuring the survival of genetic information.

There is nothing in principle wrong with the evolutionary
psychologist's analysis *so far as it goes*. Indeed, it should not
surprise us that love has adaptive value for the survival of individuals and the species. Where these analyses go askew, and
what contributed to Price's demise, is the errant assumption that
because love can be analyzed from the perspective of evolutionary psychology (e.g., as an emotional attachment with biological
value), that love is *nothing but* an emotional attachment with
biological value. That clearly doesn't follow.

While researchers in general are not committed to this re-
ductive analysis, *atheistic researchers are*. From a perspective
consistent with their metaphysics, love really is *nothing but*
biologically advantageous emotional attachment, or what an
English professor once cynically defined as "two people agree-
ing to use one another." This is reductionism run amok. Love

may have biologically adaptive value, but love is not simply to be identified with that biologically adaptive value. To the extent that you recognize love is something more than biologically advantageous emotional attachment, to the extent you recognize it is as surely an objective part of our universe as gravity or matter, to that extent you have a reason to count atheism false.

In the Christian analysis, the most basic love is *agape* love, and *agape* is love unapologetically defined apart from any biologically adaptive payoff. *Agape* is the desire for the other to achieve *shalom*, or well-being, irrespective of any value one personally derives in the other achieving that *shalom*. The fundamental beauty and transcendent reach of *agape* is found in the fact that it doesn't conform to the baser biological instincts for survival.

My point is not that atheists cannot show love generally or *agape* specifically. In fact, I think John does show it in his unwavering concern for the weak and indigent. The problem, rather, is that he has no analysis of it from within the restrictive confines of his worldview. Herbert Simon infamously categorized the altruism of people like Mother Teresa from an evolutionary psychological perspective as "bounded rationality." In other words, Simon believes that when people show concern for the weak and indigent, they are not acting wisely (in other words, they're being foolish) because the only kind of love worth mentioning is that which has an evolutionary benefit.[4] This is the first debate in which I am forced to disagree with John because I don't want him to be stupid. I want his loving concern for the weak and indigent to be not an instance of bounded rationality but a concern for the *shalom* of others that is rooted in the image he bears and the God that image reflects.

▶ John's Opening Statement

Randal is an expert at playing games with words, but these games solve nothing significant. Nearly all of Randal's chosen debate topics (except chapters 17 and 19), if shown correct, would not present the slightest problem for most of the people on the planet. They have no force at all against non-Christian theisms that disagree with his particular type of Christian faith, which includes *biblical theisms* such as Islam or Orthodox Judaism, and *nonbiblical theisms* such as Hinduism, polytheism, and Deism. Nor do they have any force against *nonnaturalist atheisms* such as Buddhism and Taoism. He still must argue for his specific trinitarian, virgin-born, incarnational, biblically centered faith.

At no point along my intellectual journey, starting out as an evangelical turned liberal turned deist, would his arguments have any force at all until the very last stage when I became a metaphysical naturalist, because up until that point I could have agreed with nearly all of them.

Even now I am not completely sure a supernatural force (or being) doesn't exist. I just don't think so, that's all. I had plenty of reasons to become a non-Christian even before I reached my present stage. I have written and edited four books on why there is no good reason for thinking Christianity is true. Of that I am sure. Whether there is some supernatural force (or being) out there is a nonissue to me because *such a distant God is no different than none at all*. Once I saw the Bible as nothing but a product of ancient barbaric, nonscientific people, there was no reason to believe in the Christian God anymore. And once I understood why I concluded as I did, I saw clearly that there were no good reasons to believe in any other religion—for the same reasons.

The only reason Randal cares about this issue is because he believes the God who exists is the same one who sent Jesus to die for him and with whom he will spend eternity. But the actual source of these additional Christian beliefs is the Bible and the theology he has built on it. What I'm doing here by contrast is showing why we cannot believe the Bible or the supposed good God it speaks about. If we have no good reason to believe the Bible or its God, then the question of whether there is a supernatural force (or being) out there is an uninteresting academic one for people only interested in that sort of thing as a curiosity. For if that's all we can conclude, and there is no way to know what this force (or being) wants us to do, why we're here, or where we're going when we die, then it ends up being an unnecessary hypothesis even if it's true. No one who believes in such a nebulous supernatural force (or being) would even care to engage in writing a book like this one. So while these debates are religiously motivated for Randal, he's defending the reliability of the source of his beliefs in the Bible only insofar as I introduce these topics in this book. My goal is to force Christians to think about what they would believe if the Bible itself was undermined as a source of divine truth. My prediction is they probably wouldn't believe at all.

What's Randal doing?

With regard to the issue of love, given the scientific fact of evolution, love is a biological impulse based on the need for survival and expressed toward our kith and kin. That we love is a biological fact of social animals like us—something we find in the animal kingdom. Konrad Lorenz was one of the three European founders of ethology (the study of the natural behavior of animals in their environments). Lorenz was co-awarded the Nobel Prize in 1973 for his preceding body of work that created this new scientific discipline. In an international bestselling work he describes the behavior of several different species, including jackdaw birds who mate for life. Lorentz compares their love favorably with that of human beings. For them like us, romance begins with "love at first sight." They have a lengthy engagement with a full courtship before they copulate, and the pair "form a heartfelt mutual defence league, each of the partners supporting the other most loyally." He writes, "Many higher birds and mammals behave in exactly the same way as the human being."[5] Do they need a God to love like they do? I think not. Neither do we.[6]

▶ Randal's Rebuttal

After a long, meandering, and irrelevant introduction, John finally gets to the topic. But he has little patience for it. Instead he continues to insist that science supports reductionism: "Given the scientific fact of evolution, love is a biological impulse based on the need for survival and expressed toward our kith and kin." John's problem is that evolution is a *biological* theory. If you wish to use it to explain love, you're doing philosophy, not science, and bad philosophy to boot.

By endorsing a reductionistic view of love, John effectively saws off the very branch he's sitting on. After all, expressing love for the weak and indigent is not behavior conducive to aiding survival. On the contrary, the lesson of evolution is that the weak are to be culled from the herd. Only if human beings have risen above mere biology to inhabit the spiritual virtue of *agape* can this care be metaphysically grounded.

I tried to help John, but he insisted on reductionism. So be it. If he refuses to avail himself of a theistic grounding of love, then he can embrace Herbert Simon's explanation; perhaps he suffers from "bounded rationality" after all.

▶ John's Rebuttal

I am offended by the suggestion that I cannot love as selflessly as Christians can. I do. Atheists do. Buddhists and Hindus do, as do Muslims and Mormons. It's like Randal never stepped outside his cloistered walls. I argue against Christianity selflessly since I think it is largely harmful to world peace and happiness. I get nothing much in return. In some ways I live on a meager income because of it.

From my perspective as a former pastor, I didn't meet a single person in the churches I served who had such an idealized, selfless, *agape*-type love. They all had hidden agendas at best—all of them, to a person. We see this plainly in the history of the church, which is a history of greed, lust, and ruthless power. Please tell us, Randal, where your idealized version of love can be found. It does not exist. It never did. Even Jesus was a self-absorbed, angry, power-seeking nationalist, if we take seriously the Gospel texts.

It doesn't matter if you say instead that non-Christians don't have a basis for selfless love, for that becomes an empty claim if no one loves that way.

▶ Randal's Closing Statement

John is offended that I suggested he cannot love like Christians. But I never said that. Rather, I pointed out that he has no metaphysical account of the love he shows to the weak apart from undermining it as bounded rationality. John then charges that Christians don't love selflessly. Whether true or not, that's irrelevant to the fact that they have a metaphysical ground to affirm *agape* love that atheists lack.

▶ John's Closing Statement

As I said, Randal is making a rhetorically empty claim devoid of real substance. Christians who think Mother Teresa is an example of selfless *agape* love are mistaken. Just read Christopher Hitchens's 1995 book *The Missionary Position: Mother Teresa in Theory and Practice.*[7]

◄ 12 ►

The Biblical God
Does Not Care Much
about Animals

Arguing the Affirmative: **JOHN THE ATHEIST**

Arguing the Negative: **RANDAL THE CHRISTIAN**

▶ **John's Opening Statement**

As I said before, a religion should be judged based on how it treats the defenseless. The animal kingdom is largely defenseless against the ultimate predators: humans.

While there are a few positive things said about animals in the Bible, over all it is uncaring and oblivious toward the pain and suffering we know that sentient animals experience. These texts need to be explained, not explained away.

After creating the world, God declared it all "good." Good for whom? Good for what purpose? To humans alone was given the right to "subdue" and have "dominion" over every living thing (Gen. 1:28 RSV). When we look at these Hebrew words, subdue literally means "to trample upon" (see Esther 7:8; Jer. 34:11; Zech. 9:15). The word dominion means to "master" over someone, especially when he or she refuses to be subdued (the same Hebrew word is used to describe ruling over slaves in 1 Kings 9:23 and Isa. 14:2). Together they confer upon mankind a dictatorial and domineering rule over a brutal world as God's viceroys, imitating a God who could be very cruel when his creatures did not submit to his rule by obeying his every command. This text in Genesis set the standard for the treatment of animals.

When God's judgment comes down on people, animals suffer along with them for their sins, as in Noah's flood, the ten Egyptian plagues, wars, and droughts.

Animal sacrifices were a completely unnecessary waste of animal life (see 2 Chron. 7:5). They did nothing to atone for anyone's sins (see Heb. 10:1–18). Their throats were slit and the blood was drained on the altar where they were subsequently skinned and quartered before being burned.

Conspicuously lacking in the Old Testament prophets are any prophetic denunciations of animal cruelty. In the New Testament the treatment of animals is actually worse. Jesus was not a vegetarian. He neglected animals when describing the two greatest commandments. Jesus commissioned his disciples to "make disciples of all nations" (Matt. 28:19; see vv. 16–20). No expressed concern for animals here! According to Jesus, at the judgment day nothing is said about being judged for not caring for animals (Matt. 25:31–46). And nothing is said in the final chapter of the book of Revelation that animals will be in the new heavenly Jerusalem either.

There was also a major shift in the eating habits of Christians in the New Testament. Unlike in the Old Testament, all animals were now considered fair game for hunting, herding, raising, and eating (Mark 7:19; Acts 10:9–16). In 1 Corinthians 9:9–10 the apostle Paul said God is not concerned with oxen. If so, he is not concerned with any other animal either.

The only positive thing in the New Testament is that with Jesus's death Christians eventually no longer sacrificed animals. But this was not something they decided out of care for animals.

My claim is that we do not see much of a concern for animals in the Bible. It truly is anthropocentric to the core. And as such, it's not indicative at all of what a perfectly good God would reveal to us. If God was truly concerned for the welfare of animals, he would have consistently said, "Thou shalt not mistreat or abuse animals." Then Western Christianized people could not justify the ill treatment of them down through the centuries.

God simply should not have created predation in the natural world; he should have made us all vegetarians or vegans. The amount of creaturely suffering in this world is atrocious as animals prey on one another to feed themselves, including humans feeding on animals.

There can be little doubt any longer that animals have central nervous systems as do humans and therefore feel pain in much the same way as we do. Andrew Linzey summarizes the evidence in these words:

> Animals and humans show a common ancestor, display similar behavior, and have physiological similarities. Because of these triple conditions, these shared characteristics, it is perfectly logical to believe that animals experience many of the same emotions as humans. . . . In fact, the onus should properly be on those people who try to deny that animals have such emotions. They must explain how, in one species, nerves act in one way and how they act completely differently in another.[1]

Arguing against animal experimentation and exploitation, Linzey writes, "Animals can never merit suffering; proper recognition of this consideration makes any infliction of suffering upon them problematic."[2] Indeed! Again, "Animals can never merit suffering." Period. It does not make a whit of difference whether human beings or God inflict this suffering upon them. There is no moral justification for it. None.[3]

▶ Randal's Opening Statement

In his book *River Out of Eden*, Richard Dawkins describes how the digger wasp lays its eggs inside a host, thereby turning its victim into a macabre incubator in which the eggs will eventually hatch and eat their way out of their quivering host. Dawkins observes, "This sounds savagely cruel but . . . nature is not cruel, only pitilessly indifferent."[4] He's right—to an extent. You see if there is no creator, then this is simply the way things are. Nature is not cruel. It is merely pitilessly indifferent to the suffering of its creatures, and the sooner we stoically come to terms with that fact the better. Consequently, the extent to which *we* feel pity or compassion for the creatures who suffer in this world is the extent to which we have failed to embrace the dizzyingly callous implications of an atheistic view of the world.

But of course we *do* care. And moreover we *should* care. We recognize intuitively that this is *not* the way things ought to be. We recognize that the suffering of creatures *is* of moral significance, and we chafe against the present order in which animals are subjected to untold miseries. However things got to be this way (the traditional realm of doctrines of the fall), we know they are not to *remain* this way. Unfortunately, atheism offers a barren wasteland for those intuitions. On an atheistic view there is simply no sense in protesting that this is not the way things ought to be. To cultivate genuine compassion for the suffering of animals within a consistently atheistic worldview is akin to cultivating rain-forest orchids in the driest desert. It can't be done.

The only way to ground the care and compassion we feel for creatures and their suffering objectively (as opposed to a mere subjective sentiment) is to point to a providential Creator. Within a Christian framework that means recognizing that creaturely suffering is part of a greater redemptive story that encompasses those very creatures. And that is precisely the perspective of the writers of Scripture. A number of biblical passages describe God's intentions to heal a broken world. One of the most striking is Romans 8:21, where Paul writes that "the creation itself will be liberated from its bondage to decay and brought into the freedom and glory of the children of God." So what does this notion of creation being liberated from bondage mean? In the next two verses Paul explains the hope of creation's liberation in analogous terms to the Christian's hope in the resurrection of the body:

> We know that the whole creation has been groaning as in the pains of childbirth right up to the present time. Not only so, but we ourselves, who have the firstfruits of the Spirit, groan inwardly as we wait eagerly for our adoption to sonship, the redemption of our bodies. (Rom. 8:22–23)

Just as we humans long for our incorruptible resurrection body when we shall be liberated from the effects of sin, so creation also longs to be liberated from the bondage of suffering, predation, death, and carnivory at that time when it takes on its own perfected, incorruptible form.

This is a good word not simply for creation on the whole but for the individual suffering creatures that populate it. In other words, as surely as we can hope for a resurrected creation (Isa. 65:17; 2 Pet. 3:13), so we can hope for resurrected creatures within that creation.[5] This amazing vision was immortalized in Isaiah's unforgettable description of the messianic age:

> The wolf will live with the lamb,
>   the leopard will lie down with the goat,
> the calf and the lion and the yearling together;
>   and a little child will lead them.
> The cow will feed with the bear,
>   their young will lie down together,
>   and the lion will eat straw like the ox.
> Infants will play near the hole of the cobra's den;
>   and the young child will put its hand into the
>   viper's nest. (Isa. 11:6–8)

So ultimately we have two rather stark choices before us. On the one hand, we can agree with the dreary view of Richard Dawkins that the suffering of animals is without moral significance. In this view such suffering is simply an inconsequential byproduct as sentient creatures are ground up in the clanking gears of a blind and meaningless process while nature cycles on endlessly toward its eventual oblivion. On the other hand, we could accept that the suffering of creation, however egregious, is part of the greater story of redemptive history—a story that brings hope, a story that invites us to work together for the liberation of all creatures as we anticipate the day when the world is at last healed and all creation sings.

▶ John's Rebuttal

The problem of animal suffering is this: If God is all powerful and perfectly benevolent, then why is there so much massive and ubiquitous suffering in the animal world? It's an internal problem for Randal's own religious beliefs. Yet he uses the all too familiar *you too* informal fallacy to skirt answering it, hoping instead for the future, even though animals have been suffering for millions of years. Is that the best God can offer them?

There is little we can do to stop a cat from toying with and then killing mice. That's just what predators like cats do. As Dawkins says, nature is indifferent toward suffering. But we are human beings, and as such we do care for animals. We care for our ecosystem. We've evolved to care for such things, and we should, especially since the future of our kith and kin on planet earth is at stake. We recoil in horror when we hear of extreme abuse of dogs or cats precisely because we are *humane* beings. Morality evolves, and it finally caught up to judge what we see in God's Bible as barbaric. It's been long overdue.

▶ Randal's Rebuttal

John avers that the Hebrew words for *subdue* (*kabash*) and *master* (*radah*) in the Genesis 1:28 creation mandate "confer upon

mankind a dictatorial and domineering rule over a brutal world."
Alas, this is a classic case of getting out of a text what you want to
find. In other words, John reads into these words the very *worst*
of human sovereigns rather than the *best*. But the text suggests
otherwise, for our ruling of creation is meant to *replenish* (*male'*)
the earth, not *oppress* it. And this can only occur when the sovereign's rule is one of nurturing care rather than callous indifference.

John's charge reeks of the irony of somebody who has not yet
come to terms with his own worldview. After all, what mandate
does he think a purposeless struggle for survival confers upon
human beings? If any worldview lacks any objective ground for
compassion to other sentient beings, it is atheism. To be blunt,
if nature really is "pitilessly indifferent," then why shouldn't
we be as well?

▶ John's Closing Statement

Randal's God created a horrific and unnecessary predatory
relationship among his creatures, and he authorized the oppression of animals. Randal needs to explain why he cares when his
God clearly doesn't. Just look into the eyes of your dog or cat
and tell me we need a God to care. We care because all sentient
animals are an intimate part of the structure of our lives.

▶ Randal's Closing Statement

John claims that I commit the *you too* fallacy. This is confused. I
don't think John has to explain why God allows animal suffering.
But he does have to explain why *we should care* about it. John's
only answer is that "we are human beings, and as such we *do* care
for animals" (emphasis added). But this is merely a psychological
description. John can't explain why we *ought* to care. By contrast,
a Christian theist objectively grounds those compassions in a
compassionate God who is working to restore his broken world.

◄ 13 ►

Everybody Has Faith

Arguing the Affirmative: **RANDAL THE CHRISTIAN**

Arguing the Negative: **JOHN THE ATHEIST**

▶ Randal's Opening Statement

At the end of his quasi-documentary *Religulous*, Bill Maher states, "Faith means making a virtue out of not thinking."[1] With this quip, Maher aligns himself with the tired tradition of opposing faith to reason—a tradition that includes many of the leading atheists today. For example, Richard Dawkins writes: "The whole point of religious faith, its strength and chief glory, is that it does not depend on rational justification. The rest of us are expected to defend our prejudices."[2] John also endorses this tendentious definition of faith when he writes on the Debunking Christianity website: "Faith doesn't need scientific evidence. It's irrational. I want everyone to think 'irrational' whenever someone says the word 'faith' because that's what it is."[3] But the most famous iteration of this faith versus reason view comes from Mark Twain when he defined faith as "believing what you know ain't true." In honor of that ignominious definition, I'll henceforth refer to this faith versus reason view as the *Twain definition*.

Those who adopt the Twain definition of faith tend to have an equally distorted view of reason. It is a view that demands that we always seek evidence, and where evidence is not available, we doubt. As W. K. Clifford put it in his famous essay "The Ethics of Belief," "It is wrong always, everywhere, and for anyone, to believe anything upon insufficient evidence."[4] Needless to say, when faith is defined as "belief without evidence" and reason is defined as "doubt without evidence," the chasm between the two cannot be greater.

The problem with Clifford's claim is that he never provides any *evidence* for it. He simply believes it and expects his readers to do so as well. Since a claim always demands evidence, Clifford's failure to meet his own standard makes the claim self-defeating: if we accept it, we ought to reject it! The same problem attends John's claim that faith doesn't need scientific evidence. Apparently *that* claim doesn't need scientific evidence since John provides none—a fact that leaves the reader suspicious that John has made a faith claim that is, by his own definition, irrational.

Clifford and John both provide good examples of what happens when you naïvely pit faith (= belief) against reason (= doubt). Buying into this dichotomy does not result in the expulsion of faith from your beliefs. Instead it merely leaves faith to sneak in through the back door unseen and unexamined. And as you can imagine, the faith that sneaks in the back door is the kind that would never be permitted through the front entrance. A case in point: Clifford and John's self-defeating claims that slip into the back because they have no evidence to pay the doorman.

In order to get beyond this impasse, we can consider philosopher Anthony Kenny's definition of reason: "The rational human being is the person who possesses the virtue that is in contrast with each of the opposing vices of credulity and skepticism."[5] That is, proper reasoning prevails by believing when it is appropriate to believe and withholding belief when it is appropriate to withhold belief. Sometimes it is wise to believe a person's testimony, but at other times (like when he or she makes arbitrary and self-defeating assertions) it is reasonable to be skeptical.

The interesting thing about Kenny's definition of reason is that it has a faith element built into it. In its essence, faith is belief coupled with trust. Even the reasonable assent to a person's testimony includes a trust (and faith) element in the veracity of the testifier. And this means that far from being opposed, faith and reason are really like two oars in a boat: Row on only one side of the vessel and you go in circles. You only really get going when you grasp both oars.

While the Twain definition may be spurious, it is nonetheless rhetorically brilliant, so I understand why atheists use it. Defining yourself as *reasonable* and everyone else as irrational "faith-heads" (as Dawkins says) is a good way to get the upper hand in debate. But faith still slips in the back door. You may say the atheist who insists "I exercise reason, not faith" is like the child who insists "I breathe air, not oxygen." To breathe the one is to breathe the other, and the speaker who insists otherwise merely reveals his ignorance of both.

▶ John's Opening Statement

There are some things I know without much doubt at all. The most certain thing I know is the cogito of René Descartes: "I think therefore I am." Could I be wrong and not really exist? I doubt it. And as long as I doubt it there is someone doing the doubting—me. There are other things I know; for instance, I know I'm typing these words and drinking some coffee while I do. (Ahhh, that tasted good.) I have no reason at all to doubt my senses and the personal experiences I'm presently having. They are incorrigible to me. Do I have faith that my coffee tastes good? No, I personally sense that it tastes good. There are other things I know without too much doubt—things too many to even list—and they are all based on solid empirical evidence along with good reasons for thinking them to be so. The more evidence and reasons there are for what I think is the case, then the more I can claim them to be the case.

When it comes to faith, there are at least two ways to understand it. First, faith as hopeful, wishful thinking, motivates us to achieve great things. It helps us win the love and affection of a lover, a sports contest, or an important award. Sometimes we must maintain it in the face of all odds; otherwise we may quit trying. This kind of faith is like a self-fulfilling prophecy. But it cannot make something come true that doesn't involve our actions. Many things are simply beyond our control. Faith can't make it true that Jesus arose from the dead. He either did or he didn't. Faith will not change these kind of facts. So when faith is used to make facts true that it cannot make true, I think faith is pretty much irrational. Wishful thinking about facts we cannot make true is not what thinking adults should do.

Faith in the second sense is always a leap beyond the probabilities, for if something is highly probable then I don't believe it to be true. I know it to be true by the degree of probability it has. We need to think exclusively in terms of probabilities and not try to add faith to them since faith doesn't add anything at all. If we did this, all that would matter would be the probabilities. There would be no need for faith. Faith in this sense means someone is accepting an improbable conclusion. So I eschew faith-based reasoning entirely and instead embrace science-based reasoning. I may be wrong in how I assess the probabilities, but I can never go against them.

Having said this, I do agree that almost everybody has faith, but this isn't a good thing. Rather, it's a problem to be overcome. According to Michael Shermer, "The brain is a belief engine."

> We form our beliefs for a wide variety of subjective, personal, emotional, and psychological reasons in the context of

environments created by family, friends, colleagues, culture, and society at large; after forming our beliefs we then defend, justify, and rationalize them with a host of intellectual reasons, cogent arguments, and rational explanations. Beliefs come first, explanations for beliefs follow. . . . Once beliefs are formed, the brain begins to look for and find confirmatory evidence in support of those beliefs, which adds an emotional boost of further confidence in the beliefs and thereby accelerates the process of reinforcing them, and round and round the process goes in a positive feedback loop of belief confirmation.[6]

Psychology professor James Alcock defines faith-based reasoning as "belief in search of data." Full stop. Think about the implications of this and you'll realize that we must cultivate doubt not faith. Doubt is, after all, the adult attitude.

Evolutionary psychologist Jesse Bering calls belief "an instinct" in that "we have a cognitive bias to see intentions in inanimate objects."[7] Pascal Boyer, professor of collective and individual memory, argues that we are "agency detectors" just like our animal predecessors who thought they saw agents, or predators, in the rustling leaves.[8] Agency detecting produced many more false alarms than actual threats to their lives, but because they had that instinct, they survived. Human beings also see agents in inanimate objects. Our human forbearers saw them in the thunder and lightning and concluded there were supernatural agent(s) above the clouds who were angry. They saw it in bumper crops and wives who gave birth to baby boys and concluded there were supernatural agent(s) who were pleased. Believers today still cannot bring themselves to think the universe was *not* created by a supernatural agent precisely because they still are agency detectors. This is the problem to overcome.

▶ Randal's Rebuttal

John defines faith in his opening statement as "accepting an improbable conclusion." Unfortunately that's yet another example of the spurious Twain definition—believing something you really *ought not* believe.

Among the things he thinks he knows, John lists the immediate deliverances of his sense experience. Why? Because, John says, "I have no reason at all to doubt my senses and the personal experiences I'm presently having." But that's not true. Sense perception often leads us astray. So the extent to which John accepts the deliverances of his senses despite possible error is *the extent to which he trusts them.* And as I said, trust plus belief *is* faith.

John still tries to meet Clifford's view of reason by claiming, "I know it [any truth claim] to be true by the degree of probability it has." That's a ridiculous statement. John doesn't do a probability calculation every time he has a sense experience. He has faith in his sense perception.

▶ John's Rebuttal

Clifford's argument is not one of deductive logic resulting in a certain conclusion; it's an inductive one. The evidence for his view is cumulatively found everywhere, leading us to an exceedingly probable conclusion. Probability is all that matters. Randal cannot slip in the mere possibility that there are things he can believe without sufficient evidence when the total weight of evidence is against such a bald-faced assertion. We need only look to the alternative proposition that people are within their epistemic rights to believe without sufficient evidence in *any other area.* That's a recipe for disaster, and Randal knows this.

Besides, what is a fact? All facts are basically theory laden. So by definition, facts require a reasoning process to see them as such. When this is understood, there can be no objection at all to Clifford if we simply understand facts as evidence plus reasoning. So following Alvin Plantinga, Randal falsely mischaracterizes Clifford by arguing that his view is self-defeating. Who in their right mind would not want sufficient evidence except someone who wants to irrationally slip their particular trinitarian, incarnational, resurrection faith in the back door? Mormons and Muslims do the same thing.

▶ Randal's Closing Statement

If we really sought to provide sufficient evidence for *every* claim, we would face an infinite regress because every piece of evidence would require additional evidence ad infinitum. The evidence doesn't support Clifford's unrestricted evidentialism. Rather, it supports the necessity of faith (belief and trust) in every belief system. And trust in John's arbitrary and self-defeating claims is not well placed.

▶ John's Closing Statement

Given cognitive faculties that are functioning properly, our senses are more than adequate to draw reasonable conclusions about our experiences. Look at the lengths Randal must go in order to slip his God through the cracks. No wonder I think he's deluded. Faith is an irrational leap over the probabilities.

◄ 14 ►

The Biblical God Is Ignorant about Science

Arguing the Affirmative: **JOHN THE ATHEIST**

Arguing the Negative: **RANDAL THE CHRISTIAN**

► John's Opening Statement

According to astrophysicist Neil DeGrasse Tyson,

> I have yet to see a successful prediction about the physical world that was inferred or extrapolated from the content of any religious document. Indeed, I can make an even stronger statement. Whenever people have used religious documents to make detailed predictions about the physical world they have been famously wrong. By a prediction I mean a precise statement about the untested behavior of objects or phenomena in the natural world that gets logged before the event takes place.[1]

So let's rehearse the things we do not find in the Bible but which should have been revealed by a good and omniscient God if he knew about them. My claim is that there is nothing in the Bible that reveals an all-knowing God, and that an all-loving one didn't reveal some things that would be helpful and compassionate toward the people he claims to love. What we find is indistinguishable from him not revealing anything at all. Everything we find in it is more credibly explained as the production of a prescientific people.

The first and most glaring problem is that God didn't know about the age and size of the universe. Genesis 1 is contrary to modern science in so many ways, as Ed Babinski points out. He decisively shows that the Israelites, like their Mesopotamian neighbors, all believed:

> The god(s) were perched on a celestial balcony, so to speak, gazing at the drama below, handing out blessings and curses to individuals and nations alike; at least that's what the people believed who built the temples, founded the priesthoods, invented holy rituals, and performed burnt offerings (so the smoke would ascend to heaven as a "soothing aroma"— see Gen. 8:21; Exod. 29:18, 25; Lev. 3:16; 6:21; and Num. 15:3, 10).[2]

I've already suggested a different way for God to have begun the first few sentences in Genesis, which would not have led to the Galileo debacle and the ensuing loss of faith for so many people since that time.

> In the beginning God created an immeasurable universe of billions of stars, some of which are billions and billions of miles away, through a process that took billions of years out of which he finally created the sun, moon, and a spherical earth that revolves around the sun. On it he created water, land, the beasts of the sea, and eventually every living thing on it through stages as one species evolved into the next one. Finally he created human beings to rule over everything he created.[3]

Beyond this, God didn't know about the scientific method, which has brought about so many good things in life and for its creatures that it's amazing he didn't say one thing about it.[4] This means God didn't know that today's scientifically literate people could not bring themselves to accept tales of a virgin birth, transfiguration, resurrection, and ascension into the sky.

There are other things God didn't know. He didn't know about vaccines. If he had revealed how to discover them, it would have been very useful to us during the most devastating outbreak of the bubonic plague known as the Black Death, which killed a third of the population of Europe in the fourteenth century. This knowledge would also have been useful to us during the nearly worldwide pandemic of Spanish Influenza (1918–20), when between 50 and 100 million people died, making it one of the deadliest natural disasters in human history. Nor did God know about penicillin. Revealing this knowledge to us could have saved millions of lives from an early death. He didn't know about anesthesia so surgeries could be done painlessly, or the dangers of bloodletting. He didn't know that drinking polluted water or that lead poisoning could kill us. He didn't know enough to warn us about eating certain poisonous plants, or to identify the various poisonous species out there whose bite or sting could kill us.

God didn't even know that if we built cities on the fault lines of the earth it would devastate the lives of millions of people down through the centuries. In fact, he should have known because he supposedly created them. Like honey to bees, these fault lines attract us because from them we derive our water and minerals as the earth opens up and gives us access to them.

The only excuse for God is that he does not exist.

▶ Randal's Opening Statement

The real question here is whether we can credibly believe that God revealed himself through a book that reflects a scientific view of the world that we no longer accept. And to be sure, we don't accept the ancient Hebrew three-storied view of the universe. The biblical writers held to an obsolete science, and the attempts of some conservative Christians to read biblical texts in a way congruent with contemporary science is naïve and harmful. The question is whether that obsolete science discredits the text's revelatory status.

This question brings us to another: If God should *not* have used ancient Israelite science when revealing himself to the ancient Israelites, then which science should he have used? I'm guessing that John thinks God should have used *our* science, making Genesis 1 read:

> In the beginning 13.7 billion years ago there was a cosmic singularity. After a period the energy cooled sufficiently and God formed subatomic particles. . . .

Yes, that's how God should have done it, with Genesis 1 and 2 introducing Big Bang cosmology, Einsteinian relativity, quantum physics, plate tectonics, and evolutionary biology. Give those ancient Israelites a *real* science education.

Alas, there are two glaring problems with this suggestion. The first is that such an account of the world wouldn't have made any *sense* to the ancient Israelites. Can you imagine people who considered a chariot cutting-edge technology trying to get their minds around $E=mc^2$? If God had revealed himself to the ancient Israelites in the science of the twenty-first century, he would have ensured their inability to understand the text.

John may reply that at least *we* would understand it. Perhaps, but this immediately leads us into the second problem. If the history of scientific progress to this point is any guide at all, scientific theories will continue to be revised year by year—sometimes to the point where they are replaced altogether. For example, it is only in the last ten years that scientists have stumbled upon dark energy—a mysterious substance that likely composes the bulk of what constitutes the universe. Even more bizarrely, some scientists are now arguing that *all matter is really a holographic projection.* This claim is linked somehow to the strange fact that black holes appear to record information about the things they consume on their surface like a magnetic strip. I don't pretend to understand this, but I do glean this lesson: while our view of the universe has things *less wrong* than the ancient Israelites, that hardly means we have things *right.* And this leads us back to the same problem. If God revealed himself in our science, then in a century people will reject the text for the same reason John rejects it today!

Forget the naïve assumption that God should have revealed himself in the science of our day. Let's refashion the atheist's objection to say that he should simply have revealed the way things are, period. For example, as we speak, scientists are searching for the grand unifying theory (or GUT) that can reconcile the four fundamental forces (the weak and strong nuclear forces, gravity, and electromagnetism) in a single, simple explanation. Let's say that this is the GUT equation: $X=qr$. So now we ask why God didn't place $X=qr$ at the beginning of Genesis 1.

Unfortunately, that suggestion encounters multiple problems. To begin with, what if we do not discover $X=qr$ for centuries or millennia to come? In that case we are suggesting that God should have privileged people in the distant future while leaving the rest of us in incomprehension. To compound the problem, what if human beings *never* discover $X=qr$? What if the calculus behind it is simply too difficult for the human brain to grasp? In that case our demands on the revelatory text would have fated it to permanent irrelevance.

Finally, even if some day far in the future a few scientists come to understand the truth of $X=qr$, does it follow that they would then accept the Bible as revelation? Hardly. No doubt many would dismiss the fact that $X=qr$ appears in the biblical text as a fluke. Indeed, since the ancient Israelites didn't know what $X=qr$ even meant, the atheist would probably claim that reading the GUT equation into the biblical text is as naïve as we consider reading contemporary cosmology into the biblical text.

Rather than fashion his revelation to meet the demands of the twenty-first-century skeptic, God entered into history by accommodating to the limited horizons of the ancient Near East while bringing a message of salvation history that would remain relevant for all people and all times.

▶ John's Rebuttal

Surely there are some things that modern science knows that the ancients did not know but which will be known by all future science. Those are the kinds of things I suggested God didn't reveal but should have. So the two problems Randal sees with my suggestions are utterly irrelevant to my point. Sorry. For instance, Einsteinian science did not discredit or undermine Newtonian science. It just added time as a fourth dimension. Newtonian science still works given that stipulation.

Not only would my suggestions make sense to the ancient Israelites, but they could confirm them with their own experiments. Then in turn it would confirm there is a God to modern scientists like Neil DeGrasse Tyson and any future scientists. Revealing this scientific knowledge to humans would keep modern, scientifically literate people from discounting God's supposed revelation in the Bible. And it would show his care and concern for his creatures too.

There is simply no way God should not have known and revealed these things, especially since not doing so discredits him in today's world. As I said, what we find in the Bible is indistinguishable from God not revealing anything at all.

▶ Randal's Rebuttal

John appears to have two objections to the ancient worldview that undergirds the Bible: (1) "there is nothing in the Bible that reveals an all-knowing God," and (2) "an all-loving one didn't reveal some things that would be helpful and compassionate toward the people he claims to love." Let's consider these points in turn.

I already dealt with the first point in my opening statement where I argued that in fact accommodation to the science of the day is precisely what we would expect if God were revealing himself to a particular people at a particular time in history. In addition, John's assumption that a revelation should include some special, scientific information fails for the reasons already noted.

What about the second point? Why didn't the Bible include some scientific information that might have made life easier? The question reveals a misunderstanding of the Bible's purpose. God's revelation in the Bible was to deal not merely with our physical condition but with our spiritual one, and it is perfectly suited to that task.

▶ John's Closing Statement

Randal's rebuttal fails to understand the kinds of things God could have revealed but didn't. God could have predicted what we would discover in each new generation, like the light bulb, the automobile, flight, space travel, and the internet. Randal also argues for an unhealthy dichotomy between spiritual salvation and a healthy existence.

▶ Randal's Closing Statement

John claims God should have revealed some kind of scientific fact—perhaps the sphericity of the earth—in the Bible even though it would have made no sense to an ancient Israelite. In other words, he wishes that the Bible had been written with him, rather than the Israelites, in mind. But as I pointed out, scientific factoids of this type would likely have been explained away regardless, thereby rendering their inclusion a moot point.

◄ 15 ►

God Is Found in the Majesty of the Hallelujah Chorus

Arguing the Affirmative: **RANDAL THE CHRISTIAN**

Arguing the Negative: **JOHN THE ATHEIST**

▶ **Randal's Opening Statement**

In his book *Climbing Mount Improbable*, atheist Richard Dawkins recounts an exchange he had with his daughter Juliet (then six) when she pointed to some flowers beside the road: "I asked her what she thought wildflowers were for. She gave a very thoughtful answer. 'Two things,' she said. 'To make the world pretty, and to help the bees make honey for us.'"[1]

Juliet's response is interesting for two reasons. To begin with, there is her innate penchant to find teleology (purpose) in the natural world—wildflowers are for helping bees. But I'll focus on her other point, the belief that the wildflowers add an objectively beautiful complement to the world. This belief depends on the assumption that objective aesthetic value exists—an assumption that has been shared by most philosophers throughout history. That is, most philosophers have agreed with Juliet's intuition that things like wildflowers really make the world objectively more beautiful than it would be otherwise.

If you disagree and think that beauty is merely in the eye of the beholder, then you are a victim of the modern age. Perhaps you think that beauty is rooted in subjective individual preference or social convention. That's a popular idea borne out of the observation that standards of beauty are, to an extent, reflective of our personal taste and cultural formation. But this observation is quite irrelevant. Even if our *perception* of that which is beautiful is shaped by preference and culture, it doesn't follow that that which is beautiful is *constituted* by preference and culture.

Despite the fact that the world evinces brokenness and pain, it is also awash with beauty of dizzying intensity. Some of it, like Juliet's wildflowers, is found in the natural world. I remember the experience of snorkeling in the Great Barrier Reef in Australia. The ride out to the coral shoal was memorable enough with the sunlight sparkling like a million diamonds on the azure tropical waters. But that was nothing compared to what I found beneath the waves: bright, vivid coral and teeming schools of fish with colors so vibrant they looked like they'd been painted by a kindergarten class gone wild.

There is also great beauty of human artifice. Think for instance of the haunting choral glory of "Agnus Dei" being performed in a grand medieval cathedral. Try to envision the soaring angelic voices rising and weaving in and out of centuries-old stone vaults and columns while candles silently flicker in the adjoining chapels, casting an ethereal glow over the sanctuary.

For centuries people have believed that such experiences represent an encounter with objective beauty. It is a curious dogma of modernity that dismisses the visceral experience of beauty we have in these moments as really nothing more than a reflection of our own subjective preferences. On the contrary, the beauty of the reef is as objective as its properties of mass and shape. Thus, the reef would exemplify that objective beauty even if human beings had never observed it. Similarly, the haunting majesty of a performance of "Agnus Dei" would remain even if the people sitting in the pews were deaf or asleep or unable to appreciate anything of greater musical sophistication than The Ramones.

Dawkins demurs. In response to Juliet's proclamation of the beauty of the wildflowers, he comments, "I was touched by this and sorry I had to tell her it wasn't true."[2] How does he know this? Because in his view, objective beauty *cannot* exist. After all, if an atheist admits the existence of objective aesthetic valuation—or what philosophers have called *the beautiful*—he is forced next to explain what *the beautiful* is such that it can be exemplified in things as diverse as tropical fish, wildflowers, and a sublime performance of "Agnus Dei."

Needless to say, *the beautiful* that befuddles the atheist fits comfortably within a Christian metaphysic. In his *fourth way* (one of five arguments for the existence of God), Thomas Aquinas points to the fact that things have a graded participation in objective qualities like goodness and beauty. The theist offers a metaphysical ground for those objective values in the one creator God insofar as things reflect his goodness and beauty. Thus it is with good reason that we sense awe when encountering truly beautiful things like the fish and coral of the reef, the wildflowers of a meadow, or a performance of "Agnus Dei." In the same way that we see the sun's light sparkling on tropical waters and illuming the world below, so we see the light of God shining on, in, and through his creation.

▶ **John's Opening Statement**

Randal's intention here is to argue for the existence of God from the supposed existence of objective aesthetic beauty.

For me, this is simple. Beauty is in the eye of the beholder. It has to be. There is no beauty in the world at all, just as there isn't anything ugly either. There is no color or sound or taste or smell or pain in the world. All that exists is raw, uninterpreted stuff. There are objects having certain shapes, objects that are made up of certain particles reflected in the periodic table of elements, and objects that are made of molecules and atoms. There are also wavelengths originating from moving objects or particles emitting from them. So seeing is dependent on a beholder. Hearing is dependent on a hearer. Smelling is dependent on a smeller. Tasting is dependent on a taster. Pain is dependent on nerve endings that send messages to brains. Even when there is a beholder, if we could see and hear the whole electromagnetic and sonic spectra, all we would be able to see and hear is white noise. Would Randal say white noise is beautiful?

What we find beautiful is largely based on our biology and thus explained by evolution. Just consider what the various animals in the world may think is beautiful. Take dogs for instance. Their olfactory senses are extremely sensitive. I saw a program in which a bloodhound was given the scent of a particular man and subsequently found the seat where that man had sat among thousands of seats in a huge stadium. But guess what smells wonderful to these dogs? Butts. Smelly, stinky butts. They stick their noses in them—especially butts of other dogs. It must smell really good to them, beautiful that is, even though with their sense of smell it must be extremely bombshell-busting strong. The silvertip grizzly bear's olfactory sense is seven times stronger than that of the bloodhound! Most all human beings with our much weaker sense of smell think that smelly butts are putrid. So is there objective beauty or not? I think not. It depends first of all on which species we're talking about.

Some dolphins, whales, and bats use echolocation to navigate and track prey by sending out sounds or waves and then receiving them back. At night many snakes use infrared organs to detect warm-blooded prey. Sharks and electric eels can detect electric fields generated by other animals in the water. Hammerhead sharks can detect half a billionth of a volt! Some birds and worker bees can detect the geomagnetic field and use it as a built-in GPS system to navigate their worlds. Jumping spiders can see not just three, but four primary colors. They have what is called *tetrachromatic* vision. The fourth color they see is ultraviolet light, which actually appears like an entire extra spectrum to them. Mantis shrimp can see even more, since they can see what jumping spiders see, but they also see polarized light. The animal kingdom has plenty of creatures whose senses go far beyond what we can experience. And so they almost certainly have a different sense of what is beautiful than we do. What then becomes of Randal's claim that there is objective aesthetic beauty?

When it comes to human beings, there is a neurologically based condition called *synesthesia* in which stimulation of one sense leads to involuntary experiences in a second sense. People with it see sounds, hear colors, and taste smells, or they smell colors, hear smells, and see sounds, depending on the person. Basically their wiring is different from most of the rest of us. Different? Yep. If we were all wired that way we would have a different sense of beauty, even as humans. There are other human conditions that exemplify this fact. Beauty is biologically based even when it comes to human beings.

Among the human species, beauty is largely culturally relative as well, even if we all agree that some things are beautiful. At best all Randal can claim is that human beings agree on that which is objectively beautiful. I suppose all dogs do too, and all mantis shrimp. So? Life on our planet originated and then evolved from a universal common ancestor. When human beings evolve into another species, then what will become of Randal's claim? Basically Randal must show that evolution is false to make this argument, but he's not doing that.

▶ **Randal's Rebuttal**

John's argument can be summarized like this:

1. Dogs like the aroma of "smelly, stinky butts."
2. Therefore, objective aesthetic facts do not exist.

There are three basic problems with this argument. First, there is a difference between liking something and finding it beautiful. For example, I generally prefer classic rock to classical music even though the latter is typically much more beautiful than the former.

Second, you cannot use the fact that people disagree with each other (and dogs) over which things are objectively beautiful to support the conclusion that nothing is objectively beautiful. It is absurd to reason from the fact that black widow spiders eat their mates to the conclusion that objective *moral* values don't exist. Similarly, it is absurd to reason from the penchant of canines to sniff butts to the conclusion that objective *aesthetic* values don't exist.

Finally, I accept neo-Darwinian evolution. But Darwinism is a theory of biological origins, not aesthetic valuation, and thus it is irrelevant to the topic.

▶ **John's Rebuttal**

I too have gone snorkeling. I did so off the coast of Cancun, Mexico. I too was amazed at what I saw. It was absolutely beautiful in the crystal-clear waters of the Caribbean Sea. I would suppose every human being would agree. So? It appears to me that Randal has never given a moment's thought to the fact that beauty is biologically based. Otherwise he would not have bothered making this argument.

Human beings have evolved to behold that which we do. And so it stands to reason that as a species we agree on what is beautiful. But it says absolutely nothing about what is objectively beautiful. We can even imagine the existence of an evolved species of aliens who visited our planet who would certainly see our world differently than us with their different sensory inputs.

Nature contains nothing but raw, uninterpreted stuff. So for Randal to say that something is beautiful even without a beholder makes no sense at all.

The bottom line is that Randal cannot get this argument off the ground. With no objective beauty comes no argument to the existence of his particular god.

▶ Randal's Closing Statement

John reasons from the premise that humans evolved to the conclusion that objective aesthetic facts don't exist. But the conclusion doesn't follow. If it did, then John would also have to accept that objective *physical* facts don't exist, and he clearly wants those. It isn't Darwinism that keeps him from recognizing objective aesthetic facts. Rather, it is his dogmatic and misbegotten commitment to atheism.

▶ John's Closing Statement

Beauty is an emotional feeling we get when looking at, tasting, hearing, or smelling some *physically* existing thing that is pleasant to us, nothing more. Randal cannot even conceive, much less produce, one thing that all species think is pleasant, so his argument to God's existence from beauty cannot get off the ground.

◄ 16 ►

The Biblical God Is Ignorant about the Future

Arguing the Affirmative: **JOHN THE ATHEIST**

Arguing the Negative: **RANDAL THE CHRISTIAN**

► John's Opening Statement

The Bible speaks often as if God doesn't know the future (Gen. 22:12; Deut. 13:3; Jer. 3:7, 19–20; 26:3; 32:35; Ezek. 12:3; and Jon. 3:10). Why then should we think there is any reason he can predict the future with certainty, especially for creatures with free will?

There are a few easily seen failed prophecies. Isaiah predicted the river Nile would dry up (Isa. 19:5–7). Isaiah predicted Damascus would cease to be a city (Isa. 17:1–2). Ezekiel predicted Nebuchadnezzar would destroy the city of Tyre (Ezek. 26:7–14) but later admitted this didn't happen (Ezek. 29:17–20). Revising his original prediction, Ezekiel predicted instead that Egypt would become desolate and that Nebuchadnezzar would conquer it (Ezek. 29:8–12, 19–20). But that too never happened. Jeremiah predicted Jehoiakim, the king of Judah, would have no successor (Jer. 36:30) even though he was succeeded by Jehoiachin, his son (2 Kings 24:6). The prophets Haggai and Zechariah both predicted in their day that Zerubbabel was the long-awaited messiah (Hag. 2:20–23; Zech. 4:6:9–13; compare Zech. 6:9–15), but this turned out to be false as well.[1]

Elsewhere I have analyzed some of the most important claims of Old Testament prophetic fulfillment in the New Testament. My challenge is this: *I defy anyone to come up with one statement in the Old Testament that is specifically fulfilled in the life, death, and resurrection of Jesus that can legitimately be understood as a prophecy and singularly points to Jesus as the Messiah using today's historical-grammatical hermeneutical method. It cannot be done.*[2]

Many of the claimed prophecies came from the so-called *messianic psalms*. But in their original contexts there is nothing about them, when reading them devotionally, that indicates they are predicting anything at all. For there to be a prediction, there must be a prophecy, and there are none in the psalms. With no prediction comes no fulfillment. When it comes to the Suffering Servant of Isaiah 53, the servant was not a redeemer messianic king at all. In Isaiah the Suffering Servant is identified with the people of Israel themselves (see Isa. 41:8–9; 42:18–24; 43:10; 44:1–2, 21; 45:4; 48:20; and especially 49:3). One must interpret this in its context. It is Israel who has suffered so much, and from out of her sufferings Israel hoped to become a light to the nations, restored by God to her former glory. When it comes to the infancy prophecies in Matthew's Gospel, Robert Miller sums up what we find.

1. He attributes meanings to the prophets that they did not intend.

2. He interprets their words in ways that are impossible in their own contexts.

3. He relates prophecies to events that never happened.

4. He invents a prophecy that did not exist.[3]

No wonder Professor C. F. D. Moule argues that Matthew's use of the Old Testament "to our critical eyes, [is] manifestly forced and artificial and unconvincing."[4] And if this is the case, then why not be skeptical of his whole Gospel since he takes these kinds of liberties with his sources?

The most serious failed prophecy is the one Jesus himself made concerning the consummation of the ages, also known as the *eschaton*, from which we get the word *eschatology*. Jesus was a failed apocalyptic prophet because the "Son of Man" did not come in his generation as he predicted—something I've already argued elsewhere in some detail.[5] In Mark 9:1 Jesus says: "Truly I tell you, some who are standing here will not taste death before they see that the kingdom of God has come with power" (see also Matt. 16:28; Luke 9:27). No amount of theological gerrymandering can escape the conclusion that Jesus was wrong. Just like every other failed end-time movement in history, his followers successively revised this original prediction by adding additional signs of that cosmological, earth-shattering event as the earlier signs were proved wrong.

But what I consider the worst ignorance of them all is what I've called the *Problem of Divine Miscommunication*.[6] If there is a loving God who knew the future of how his sincere followers would inflict so much pain, oppression, and death on others, then he should have been very clear from the beginning about how they should act. He should have unequivocally condemned slavery, the oppression of women, and the abuse of animals. But he didn't.

God also should have specified more completely what Christians should believe doctrinally. But because he didn't, eight million Christians killed each other in the wars following the Protestant Reformation over issues most Christians today think are silly.

▶ Randal's Opening Statement

Once you have reason to believe a man named Dave is a police officer, you automatically have reason to believe Dave can operate a firearm, even if you have never seen him handle one. The reason is simple: being a police officer requires the ability to operate a firearm. Therefore, if you have reason to believe Dave is a police officer, you have reason to believe he can operate a firearm.

By the same token, if you have reason to believe that Yahweh is God, then you have reason to believe Yahweh is omniscient (that is, Yahweh knows all true propositions and believes no false ones, including propositions about the future). The reason is simple: to be divine is to be omniscient. (The property of being God entails the property of being divine.) Thus, if Yahweh is God, then he is omniscient.

One may take issue with this argument by claiming either that the concept of divinity does not necessarily include omniscience or that it is not reasonable to believe Yahweh is God. I'll respond briefly to each of these claims.

Let's begin with the definition of divinity. It is true that many people have attributed the property of divinity to beings that were very far from perfect. The Greek pantheon perched atop Mount Olympus was full of such "deities" who demonstrated character faults so glaring that they make the cast of your favorite soap opera look like paragons of virtue by comparison. But the fact that the concept of divinity has been predicated of such individuals begs the question of whether it is *proper* to apply the concept to those individuals.

In fact, Greek philosophy was borne out of the recognition that this is *not* an adequate concept of the divine. Philosophers like Plato and Aristotle concluded that the concept of divinity should not be applied to agents merely because they are immortal or very powerful. It should be reserved for a truly exalted entity, one who was variously defined as the *Form of the Good*, *Pure Act*, or a *Logos* who guides all things in their logical course.

The same process of conceptual clarification is evident in the Hebrew Scriptures, which witness the move from polytheism to monolatrism (worship of one god among many, a position that begins with Abraham) to henotheism (recognition of one God supreme over other gods, a position that begins with the exodus) to monotheism (a doctrine that is affirmed in Deutero-Isaiah, see especially Isa. 44:6).

With divinity having been identified in monotheistic terms (there is one God), the process of conceptual clarification then turned to unpacking the qualitative nature of this one divine being. The apogee of this process came with Anselm's formulation of the ontological argument, which is as much a definition *of* God as a proof *for* God. God, by Anselm's reckoning, is that being whom none greater can be conceived. In other words, God necessarily contains all perfections, and since omniscience is a perfection, God is necessarily omniscient. Thus a Christian who accepts the end results of this long and rigorous process of conceptual clarification can say unapologetically that the concept of divinity includes the property of being omniscient as surely as the concept of being a bachelor includes the property of being male.

This brings us to our next question. What reason has a Christian to believe that Yahweh is God? Let's ask another question: What reason may we have to believe Dave is a police officer? One obvious way is through testimony—somebody you know and trust *told* you that he's a police officer. Is it possible that we can likewise come to know Yahweh is God through the written or spoken testimony of another? There is no principled objection to this possibility, and so it is indeed possible to know Yahweh is God through testimony. But there are other ways as well. For example, if you prayed to Yahweh and that prayer was answered (see chapter 17), that would provide prima facie support that Yahweh is God. After all, according to Ockham's razor (do not multiply entities beyond necessity), it is simpler to posit Yahweh as the deity answering prayer rather than posit him as a subordinate agent to a deity. The same reasoning applies to those who become persuaded that Yahweh raised Jesus from the dead (see chapter 19).

In these and many other ways Christians can come to believe that Yahweh is God just as they may come to believe Dave is a police officer. And in the same way that Dave's identity as a police officer supports the conclusion that Dave can operate a firearm, so the identity of Yahweh as God supports the conclusion that Yahweh is omniscient.

▶ John's Rebuttal

This is one of the best things Randal has written in this book. Bravo!

My claim is that as religious people became aware of a bigger world, then their conceptions of God became bigger too, which is adequately described by Randal as moving from polytheism to monolatrism to henotheism to monotheism. Later, as the Western world began interacting with the Eastern world, Anselm defined God as the "greatest conceivable being," which went beyond a mere localized kind of monotheism. So just like morality, God concepts have evolved too.

One problem though is that Anselm's God is emphatically not reflected in the Bible, as I'm explaining in this book. On this topic the biblical data shows that God does not know the future. Period. That should be the end of the story. Another problem is that contrary to Anselm, an adherent of eastern religion believes *the One* (i.e., the greatest being possible) cannot be conceived, and as such is beyond comprehending. At that point Anslem's ontological argument cannot even get off the ground.

And once again Randal points out another mere possibility, that we can know his God exists because of human testimony, even though it is unreliable. Sure, this is a possibility. But *probability* is all that matters.

▶ Randal's Rebuttal

John doesn't dispute the notion that deity essentially includes omniscience, but he does claim that Yahweh is not a credible candidate for being divine because Yahweh fails to demonstrate knowledge of the future.

Is the evidence John provides sufficient to overturn one's belief that Yahweh is God? That depends on the evidence one has for thinking that Yahweh is God and the evidence John provides for thinking Yahweh is not omniscient. I cannot survey the evidence for the first claim here, but we can consider John's evidence for the second.

To begin with, John points to passages that speak of God's ignorance of certain future events. But Christian theologians interpret these as anthropomorphisms. Next, John points to alleged failed prophecies. But even if I granted every one of these, they would only point to the failure of a *human prophet*. Third, John alleges that Jesus wrongly predicted the arrival of the *eschaton*. Again, even if I granted the point, it would only mean that Jesus, in his incarnate *kenosis*, made a mistaken prediction about the future. Finally, John alleges sweeping divine miscommunication. But God could have all sorts of reasons for communicating with creation in the way he does apart from being ignorant of the future. To sum up, John provides poor evidence to think Yahweh is not omniscient, particularly if one already has independent grounds to believe Yahweh is God.

▶ John's Closing Statement

Theologians reinterpreted the biblical descriptions of God anthropomorphically as their God got bigger. To admit there are false prophecies in the inspired Bible grants way too much. There isn't a way to make coherent someone who is 100 percent God and 100 percent man anyway. And once again Randal punts to a mere possibility.

▶ Randal's Closing Statement

John admits that a Christian *could* know that Yahweh is God through testimony. He just doesn't think this is *probable*. Yet he has never presented a formal probability calculation to support his claims. Thus all John really offers are subjective intuitions cloaked in the rhetoric of *probabilities*.

◄ 17 ►

God Best Explains the Miracles in People's Lives

Arguing the Affirmative: **RANDAL THE CHRISTIAN**

Arguing the Negative: **JOHN THE ATHEIST**

► Randal's Opening Statement

Archbishop of Canterbury William Temple once observed, "When I pray coincidences happen, and when I do not pray coincidences do not happen."[1] Many Christians can resonate with Temple's wry reference to God's providence. But atheists demur, charging that such experiences only evince a selection bias that *counts the hits* and *ignores the misses*. So who is right? To answer that question we'll consider a specific case from a personal friend of mine, Kent Sparks, Professor of Biblical Studies at Eastern University.

Kent was a pastor living with his wife, Cheryl (a physical therapist), in North Carolina when they were pursuing an adoption through a crisis pregnancy ministry named House of Ruth in Downey, California. But since they had not had success with House of Ruth over the previous year and a half, they proceeded to close on a private adoption in Georgia. After they closed on the adoption of their daughter Emily and returned to North Carolina, Kent called House of Ruth and left a message requesting the agency to suspend their file. Little did Kent know that at that very moment the House of Ruth staff was in a meeting with a young woman who chose their file for her child. As soon as the meeting ended, a staff member called the Sparks to inform them of the good news. Cheryl answered the phone, assuming they were returning Kent's call. Needless to say, she was shocked to learn instead that they were calling to offer a second child for adoption! Overwhelmed by the prospect of accepting a second infant, Cheryl called a friend to ask for prayer. Later when Kent arrived home from work, Cheryl asked him to conduct a family devotion without informing him of the situation. Perplexed, Kent opened his Bible and read from Proverbs 3:27: "Do not withhold good from those to whom it is due, when it is in your power to act." Shortly thereafter Cheryl's friend called her and said, "I have a verse for you." She then quoted Proverbs 3:27. Based on that collocation of events, Kent and Cheryl accepted the adoption and welcomed their second daughter, Cara, into the family.

Is it reasonable for Kent and Cheryl (and us) to believe that this adoption was divinely endorsed? In order to answer this question we should consider the concept of a design filter.[2] When we seek to identify agency as an explanation for an event, we first seek to establish that the event was contingent. Thus, an event that is a known result of natural law is not explained via design. (That's why we don't invoke Jack Frost to explain the frost on our window panes.) Next, we need to eliminate the possibility of chance. We do that by looking for events that are sufficiently complex and specified to a situation. If the event is contingent, complex, and specified, then a design explanation for the event is warranted.

To illustrate, imagine that Fred Smith passes a movable type sign every day on his drive to work. On the day of his fortieth birthday the sign says "Happy Birthday!" Could Fred reasonably believe that the message was put there to wish *him* a happy birthday? That depends. The first hurdle to clear is an analogue of contingency. For example, if the sign *always* said "Happy Birthday!" then no design inference would be warranted. But if this was the first day that the message appeared on the sign, then the event could be considered contingent. From here the more complex and specified the message, the stronger the evidence is that it's for Fred. Thus a sign that reads "Happy Birthday Fred!" offers better evidence, while one that reads "Happy Fortieth Birthday Fred Smith!" offers excellent evidence.

Kent and Cheryl's case evinces these same hallmarks of contingency, complexity, and specification. While these events are obviously contingent, they are also complex since they involved multiple factors timed together (e.g., Kent's call concurrent with the adoption meeting), and they included specified information (e.g., two independently confirmed references to Proverbs 3:27). Consequently, Kent and Cheryl (and we) are fully justified in drawing the conclusion of divine action in confirmation of the adoption.

Do things change if we also *count the misses*? No. Fred may have never before seen a message on the sign relevant to him, but on the one day that it says "Happy Fortieth Birthday Fred Smith!" he justifiably believes the message is for him. Likewise, even if Kent and Cheryl have never had another experience like this, the contingency, complexity, and specification of *these* events are sufficient for the Sparks to believe God affirmed Cara's adoption.

▶ John's Opening Statement

Almost every scientific study done on prayer has shown that prayers are not statistically answered any better than luck.[3]

Research has shown us that people are prone to misjudge the true probabilities for any given event—we're often wrong. Take a deep breath right now. Mathematician John Allen Paulos asks us to consider the odds of whether we have just inhaled a molecule that came out of Caesar's mouth when he said, "You too Brutus?" You'll probably doubt this, but he shows that the odds of this happening stand at about 99 percent.[4]

The fact is that incredible coincidences are common, even virtually certain, given enough opportunities for them to occur in the lives of millions of believers. The most we can say about them is that their causes are unknown. So once again Randal is arguing from the gaps—a known, informal fallacy. We should not trust personal anecdotal evidence when it comes to answered prayers, especially since believers count the hits and discount the misses due to a thousand qualifications. Besides, believers in each era will only pray for things they expect can happen, and what they expect depends on the state of contemporary science. Still, the question remains why they have to ask their God for anything at all if he really cares for them as a mother cares for her children. I see no reason why they should.

Even if Christians receive an answer to a prayer, this doesn't show their particular God exists, since a different god may have answered it out of compassion. And if in reverse, the Christian God is answering the prayers of other believers in hell-bound false religions out of compassion, then God is helping to send them to hell by providing confirming evidence for their faith against Christianity.

When it comes to miracles due to prayer, it gets worse. Believing in them demands a nearly impossible double burden of proof. What believers must show is that a miracle could not have happened within the natural world because it was nearly impossible (or else it's not considered miraculous). Then they must turn right around and claim such an impossible event probably took place anyway. The probability that a miracle actually took place is inversely proportional to the probability that such an event could take place (i.e., the less probable it is that a miracle could take place, then the more probable it is that it didn't take place), so the improbability of a miracle claim defeats any attempt to show it probably happened. That's why extraordinary claims of miracles demand a greater amount of solid evidence for them (e.g., if a person tells us he levitated, we need more than just his testimony to believe him).

There is one way to evaluate the reliability of human testimony to miracles, and it comes from the findings of the Catholic Church. Dr. Matt McCormick asks us to consider the millions of miracle claims alleged by believers in Lourdes, France:

> The Catholic Church has officially recognized sixty-seven of them. A rough estimation of the general reliability of human miracle testimony from Lourdes comes out to be a mere .0000167. That is, in general, when humans give miracle testimony, their reliability is orders of magnitude worse than it needs to be for us to even provisionally accept it.[5]

While I would want to investigate personally the sixty-seven cases this believing church concluded were miracles, it still shows that we have every reason to be skeptical when believers claim a miracle took place. Moreover, since I have never seen one, I am within my rights to doubt them all. Believers have built in biases to accept miracles because they have a need to believe them. It basically shows us that people are still agency detectors—something we inherited from our animal ancestors. Since we know this about ourselves, it should cause us to be skeptical that there are agents behind unexplained events.

That there are some unexplained events I'll admit, just as there are some good things said in the Bible concerning women and animals. But the bad things must be explained and not just explained away.

This raises the problem of suffering (or evil). There is no excuse for a good God not to do miracles for the millions of believers who suffer intensely around the world. For every personal claim of a miracle healing, there are perhaps hundreds of thousands of people who receive no such thing.

▶ **Randal's Rebuttal**

John avers that "incredible coincidences" occur on a regular basis. True, and the design filter screens out events if they are merely improbable. It only triggers when an event is highly improbable *and* specified to the situation, like the sign wishing Fred a happy fortieth birthday or the collocation of events confirming that the Sparks should adopt Cara.

John protests that events like this don't establish that the deity of one's personal faith caused them. This is surely a desperate point. If I pray to the Christian God and the prayer is answered, why should I think any other being answered it? Finally, John claims that a Christian can only infer divine action if no possible natural cause could have produced the effect. This is false. A chain of chance natural causes *could* have spelled out "Happy Fortieth Birthday Fred Smith!" on the sign, but the most *plausible* explanation is still an intelligent cause. John has utterly failed to establish that one cannot reason similarly in the cases of answered prayer.

▶ **John's Rebuttal**

What Randal describes is personal anecdotal evidence that no scientist would ever accept as evidence, since incredibly improbable events happen to people all of the time. They are even *virtually certain to happen to someone sometime* given enough opportunities for them to occur in the lives of millions of believers. The really surprising thing isn't that these events happen but that they don't happen more often.

How we test prayer scientifically is what the *American Heart Journal* did when testing for answered prayer on patients who had heart bypass surgery.[6] The patients were separated into three groups. Group 1 received prayers and didn't know it. Group 3 received prayers and did know it. Group 2 received no prayers and didn't know it (science must have a control group like this representing the *null hypothesis*). Groups 1 and 3 were prayed for by various congregations throughout America. The results were very clear. There was no difference between the patients who were prayed for (groups 1 and 3) and those who were not prayed for (group 2). Moreover, the patients who knew they were being prayed for suffered significantly more complications than those who did not know they were being prayed for.

▶ Randal's Closing Statement

What John dismissively refers to as "personal anecdotal evidence" is vetted testimony—a type of evidence that is treated as of great value in a court of law, so why not here? Instead of addressing the logic of the design filter, John bewails my alleged failure to count *misses*. That's an ironic complaint since *his arguments prevent him from ever counting hits.*

▶ John's Closing Statement

We do indeed have a *design filter* preprogrammed into us from our animal ancestors to see agents behind improbable events given the proper circumstances. We are also not good at predicting the actual probabilities of an improbable event. So we should not trust personal anecdotal evidence but instead trust the scientific studies on prayer.

◄ 18 ►

The Biblical God
Is an Incompetent Creator

Arguing the Affirmative: **JOHN THE ATHEIST**

Arguing the Negative: **RANDAL THE CHRISTIAN**

► John's Opening Statement

Sam Harris tells us that "examples of unintelligent design in nature are so numerous that an entire book could be written simply listing them."[1] He's right!

Evolution cannot start something over. All it can do is select the next best thing available for survival. We see this in the human spine, which is an ineffective solution for supporting our weight as upright creatures because standing puts a huge strain on it. But that's how evolution worked out a solution for creatures who found that standing on two legs was better than being on all four—because doing so aids in food gathering, hunting, and running from predators.

We see this best in the human brain. David J. Linden, professor of neuroscience at John Hopkins School of Medicine, tells us the human brain "is, in many respects, a true design nightmare . . . built like an ice cream cone with new scoops piled on at each stage of our lineage." The human brain "is essentially a Rube Goldberg contraption."[2] Gary Marcus, professor of psychology at New York University, describes our brain as a kluge (kludge). A kluge "is a clumsy or inelegant—yet surprisingly effective—solution to a problem."[3] Just picture a house constructed in several stages by different contractors at each stage and you can get the picture. Without starting all over with a completely new floor plan, we get a kluge.

Because this is how evolution works, we have three brains built on top of one another that do different things: the hindbrain (or reptilian brain), the midbrain (the limbic system) and the forebrain (the neocortex). Because of this, it affects how we think. Marcus shows us in detail how it adversely affects our memories, beliefs, choices, language, and pleasure. He argues: "If mankind were the product of some intelligent, compassionate designer, our thoughts would be rational, our logic impeccable. Our memory would be robust, our recollections reliable."[4] But this is not what we find because of how our brains evolved.

In this same manner evolution produced the back of our throats containing both the esophagus (for swallowing) and larynx (for breathing); the relatively short rib cage, which does not fully protect most internal organs; our eyes, which are wired backward; and the male prostate gland, which in one of every two males at some point blocks the flow of urine. We have vestigial organs that no longer perform the function for which they evolved, such as the appendix, a tail (the coccyx), and tiny muscles attached to each hair follicle, which cause our hairs to stand up. We have a few thousand nasty dormant vestigial genes, the worst of which are called *endogenous retroviruses*.

Consider also all of the naturally caused suffering in our world, such as floods, tsunamis, droughts, fires, famines, volcanic eruptions, earthquakes, tornados, and monsoons. There are heat waves, blizzards, and hurricanes. There are poisonous species like the black widow spider, brown recluse spider, cobra, rattlesnake, scorpions, and many parasites, some of which are lethal and kill one person every ten seconds. There are poisonous plants including lethal ones like the autumn crocus, castor bean, daffodil, hyacinth, hydrangea, jimson weed, lily of the valley, mistletoe, morning glory, wild mushrooms, hemlock, sumac, white snakeroot (which was one of the most common causes of death among early settlers in America), and English yew, which is one of the deadliest plants on the planet (eat it and you die within minutes—there is no antidote). There are chronic diseases like cancer, emphysema, leukemia, cardiac problems, lupus, arthritis, and diabetes. We suffer from allergies, colds, migraines, Alzheimer's disease, anemia, asthma, bronchitis, colitis, Crohn's disease, epilepsy, gallstones, gastritis, glaucoma, gout, abnormal blood pressure, kidney stones, chicken pox, small pox, polio, Parkinson's disease, psoriasis, strokes, sudden infant death syndrome, thrombosis, tumors, typhoid fever, ulcers, Lou Gehrig's disease, Lyme disease, malaria, rabies, rickets, Rocky Mountain spotted fever, tuberculosis, diphtheria, leprosy, measles, meningitis, mumps, pneumonia, rubella, syphilis, shingles, scoliosis, whooping cough, Down syndrome, hemophilia, Huntington's disease, muscular dystrophy, sickle cell anemia, Tay-Sachs disease, AIDS, infertility, and so on. Major epidemics have decimated us, like the ones occurring in the years AD 542, 1331, 1556, and 1918. There are birth defects that include people born with two heads, with deformed limbs, blind, deaf, mute; and people born with mental deficiencies including dementia, bipolar disorder, and paranoid schizophrenia.

There is much more I could add, but thinking people get the point. There isn't an intelligent designer. Even if Randal still believes there is one anyway, this supernatural force (or being) is not a benevolent one, much less an omnibenevolent one. To argue that this is all Eve's fault in Eden is scapegoating.

▶ Randal's Opening Statement

John believes that if God created the universe then he is incompetent. Come again? This entire cosmos was brought into existence out of nothing approximately 13.7 billion years ago and is governed by surprisingly elegant natural laws finely tuned to a staggering degree of precision. The observable universe, which has been expanding ever since that moment of creation, is presently an incomprehensibly distant 46 billion light years to the visible edge. It is composed of over 100 billion galaxies, each far larger than we can fathom. Our own home, the Milky Way, contains over 200 billion stars and is so large that it takes 100,000 light years for light to cross it (light travels at 300,000 km per second).

One gets the faintest glimpse of its vastness and majesty by contemplating the Hubble Deep Field—an image created by compiling multiple images from the Hubble Space Telescope. There are about three thousand smudges of light in the image that was drawn from one region of the constellation Ursa Major. And almost every one of those faint smudges is a galaxy more distant than we can imagine despite the fact that it is practically in our cosmic backyard. The universe is unbelievably austere in its size and age and of awe-inspiring beauty and endless mystery. It is little surprise then that the contemplation of its majesty leaves people struggling for words. The psalmist said it well long ago: "The heavens declare the glory of God; the skies proclaim the work of his hands" (Ps. 19:1). To sum up, the universe transcends our wildest imaginations in every conceivable way including size, age, beauty, diversity, mystery, and complexity. And the Creator is incompetent *how* exactly?

I presume that the charge of incompetence is really reflective of incredulity toward the pains of planet earth, a planet where the glory of creation brought forth sentient creatures who have at times suffered greatly. This presents us with a problem of evil that every theist must take seriously. While the problem of evil *is* difficult, it is also important to keep it in perspective. To dismiss God as an incompetent creator based on your experiences on planet earth is tantamount to dismissing the president of the United States as an incompetent leader based on the cleanliness of a single bathroom tile at Chicago's O'Hare Airport. This kind of charge smacks of an indefensibly narrow-minded provincialism and anthropocentrism. Indeed, it appears to be the height of hubris to make sweeping judgments about the Creator's competence based merely on our experience on this infinitesimal pale blue dot called earth.

Perhaps it is a gross exaggeration to charge God with cosmic incompetence based on the suffering on planet earth. Nonetheless the atheist may retort that it is still reasonable to inquire as to why our particular planet has the degree of misery it does. Granted, the earth is a microscopic speck in the vast universe, but could we still not have expected better from the creator of this microscopic speck?

This objection appears to be driven by the following assumption: The amount and intensity of evil and suffering on planet earth is so great that God could not possibly have a reason for allowing it. Consequently, in virtue of allowing it, God is properly deemed incompetent.

The problem with the objection is that the objector simply lacks the broader perspective necessary to make it. He is simply too limited in time and space to say with any conviction that God really ought to have done things differently. Consider a cinematic illustration of the point: Imagine that you are attending the screening of a film that was directed by the foremost critically acclaimed director in history. After watching one minute of the three-hour film, the director's magnum opus, you are perplexed. That first minute had some great moments, incredible acting, and awesome cinematography. But the first minute also included dialogue and plot points that were so perplexing to you that they left you rethinking the competence of the director.

So what should you think? You may have some legitimate concerns based on that first minute. But would you have enough information to say that the curious dialogue and plot points of that first minute could not be redeemed and explained over the next three hours of the film? Surely it would be the height of hubris to judge the competence of the famous director based on your limited sampling of that first minute. How much more is it gross hubris to judge the Creator's competence based on something closer to a microsecond sampling of his cosmic story?

▶ John's Rebuttal

What planet does Randal live on? If God is an omnipotent creator, then why is the vast majority of the universe and our planet uninhabitable by life of any kind, much less human life? Why do the life forms that exist suffer so much if God is good? And if God could not create a better world, then why doesn't he perform perpetual miracles to alleviate our most intense sufferings?

Randal is taking an irrational leap over the probabilities. A good, intelligent creator should show he cares for each individual on this planet. If he does not, we can reasonably conclude he either does not care or he does not exist at all.

He's punting to God's omniscience as an answer—something other theists do to save their own omniscient God from refutation, making faith unfalsifiable. This proves once again that believers must be convinced their faith is nearly impossible before they will consider it improbable, which is an unreasonable standard. Even if God is omniscient and has higher ways than us, we still must know enough of his ways to know that he exists and that he cares for us—and if omniscient, he should know this about us.

▶ Randal's Rebuttal

John's argument is as provincial as I suspected. He is confident that his microsecond viewing of the film has equipped him to judge the competence of the director. He assumes that

154

no competent creator would design a less than optimal world. This is like assuming that no intelligent driver traveling from San Francisco to Los Angeles would ever take coastal Route 1 since the interstate is so much quicker. But sometimes the journey is as important as the destination. How could the less than optimal design of our planet's creatures be formative for the journey? It is tough to say, but John's microsecond viewing has not equipped him to judge the Creator's competence.

John claims that since extraordinarily complex systems like the human brain were not designed optimally, we should not believe they were designed at all. That's like looking at the interior of an old Alfa Romeo Spyder, finding the gear shifter placed where the air conditioning controls should be (Alfas are notorious for bad ergonomics) and concluding that the car had no designer. Less than optimal design, like a winding coastal highway, can exist for multiple purposes without warranting doubt of the designer's competence, let alone his existence.

▶ John's Closing Statement

None of Randal's analogies work. We have every right to judge the United States president even if *all we ever observed was that bathroom tile, because that's all we would know.* Likewise, we can't know in advance that the film director is competent, or that our journey is as important as the destination, or that there is an intelligent Alfa Romeo Spyder designer.

▶ Randal's Closing Statement

John likes to talk about *probabilities*, but that's just the way he refers to what he thinks is probable. How does John *calculate* the probability that the suffering on our planet couldn't be for some greater purpose? He doesn't. All he does is repeat his subjective opinion based on a microsecond of viewing the film.

◄ 19 ►

Jesus Was Resurrected, So Who Do You Think Raised Him?

Arguing the Affirmative: **RANDAL THE CHRISTIAN**

Arguing the Negative: **JOHN THE ATHEIST**

► Randal's Opening Statement

What would it take to persuade you that your brother is the long-expected messiah? Quite a lot I suspect. You grew up with the guy. You saw him scrape his knee, get a cold, and accidentally knock Mom's favorite vase on the floor. Is it any wonder that thinking of your sibling as the messiah strains your credulity far beyond the breaking point?

So it should be little surprise that Jesus too was met with skepticism from his siblings. To begin with, the Gospels give no evidence that the siblings of Jesus supported him during his ministry. If anything, in Matthew 12:46–50 Jesus marginalized family, placing them on the outside while his disciples were on the inside. Even more explicitly, John 7:2–5 avers that the brothers of Jesus openly *rejected* his teaching:

> But when the Jewish Festival of Tabernacles was near, Jesus' brothers said to him, "Leave Galilee and go to Judea, so that your disciples there may see the works you do. No one who wants to become a public figure acts in secret. Since you are doing these things, show yourself to the world." For even his own brothers did not believe in him.

This is hugely significant. According to the criterion of embarrassment in assessing ancient historical claims, any testimony that is embarrassing to one's cause is more likely to be true because it would not have been included otherwise. So it seems highly unlikely that the general incredulity of the brothers of Jesus toward his teaching and ministry would have been included if it had not been true. As a result, the evidence supports the fact that James was not a disciple of Jesus during his brother's life and ministry.

This makes it all the more incredible that after the death of Jesus, James emerged as the de facto leader of the Jerusalem Christians (see Acts 15:13; 21:18; Gal. 1:19; 2:9, 12). This testimony is confirmed in Jewish historian Josepheus's work *Antiquities* where he observes that James was martyred in Jerusalem in AD 62.[1]

But how did this happen? How did an intelligent man (you don't become a leader of the Jerusalem Christians without being intelligent) become persuaded that his crucified brother was the Messiah? Deuteronomy 21:23 teaches that "anyone hung on a tree is under God's curse" (NRSV). If anything, James would have viewed the crucifixion as a confirmation of his suspicions. And yet inexplicably, he became a leader of the Christians.

Paul explains why in 1 Corinthians 15 (written ca. AD 50–51), where he recounts a teaching he had received from others: "For what I received I passed on to you as of first importance" (1 Cor. 15:3). This is technical, rabbinic phrasing. One does not innovate or embellish rabbinic teaching but instead passes it on faithfully.

What was it that Paul received? He explains: Christ died, was buried, and was raised. And "raised" here is clearly a bodily resurrection, which is made abundantly clear in the rest of the chapter (as well as in the background Jewish worldview of the time). Next, Paul lists in this teaching several names of those who witnessed the risen Jesus and thereby became converts to him, including James, the brother of Jesus.

What is the best explanation for James's belief that he had seen his brother raised? Obviously legend is not a plausible explanation. There simply is no time for a legend to develop here, and James's own leadership in the church and martyrdom attests to his belief. One may think that James saw a vision, but remember, he believed his brother died under God's curse. *Visions* come within a climate of background expectation. A hypnotist or magician doesn't call the scowling skeptic in the audience up on stage. He chooses the fawning fan on the edge of her seat, ready to be manipulated. So James was definitely not susceptible to seeing a vision.

So then what? Did James get pulled into an elaborate conspiracy? To what end? So that he could be martyred?

The historian who seeks to reconstruct past events based on available evidence needs something to work with here. If you want to posit a non-miraculous reconstruction of the events you can do so, but it has to work with all the available data and be plausible. For those not closed a priori to the invocation of miraculous causes, the bodily resurrection of Jesus remains the most plausible explanation for the transformation of James. Consider it this way: My brother is a fine chap. But to believe he's the Messiah? That would take nothing short of a miracle.

▶ John's Opening Statement

Paul is the only New Testament writer who claimed he saw the risen Jesus, and his letters are the earliest testimony we have of it. But we have serious difficulties in knowing what he saw. On the Damascus Road he never claimed to have actually seen or touched Jesus (see Acts 9; 22; 26; Gal. 1). He specifically said it was a visionary experience (Acts 26:12–19; see 9:17) and that he had many of them (2 Cor. 12:1–7; see 1 Cor. 9:1). Paul even claimed he got his gospel from a private revelation (Gal. 1:11–12; which is contrary to 1 Cor. 15:3). The book of Acts tells us of Paul's visions in 16:9–10; 18:9; 22:17–18; 23:11; and we see one in Galatians 2:2. Paul repeatedly spoke of *revelations* that he passed down to the church (1 Cor. 2:13; 7:40; 14:37). He even said he learned about the Lord's Supper from the Lord himself (1 Cor. 11:23–25), which provided the basis for the stories later told in the Gospels. People in Paul's early churches were visionaries too, reflected in Acts 2:17: "Young men will see visions." They were convinced they were receiving divine messages from Jesus and expressed them through the spiritual gifts of divine "wisdom," "knowledge," "prophecy," and "tongues" (2 Cor. 12:7–10). These are private, subjective experiences. Why should anyone who did not have one accept them as reliable testimony? I see no reason why we should. Paul equated his own visionary experience of the risen Jesus with the witnesses in 1 Corinthians 15:3–8, so their testimony cannot be considered any better than Paul's.

Consider instead the gold plates Joseph Smith claimed the angel Moroni led him to discover, which he supposedly translated, producing the Book of Mormon. Smith carefully chose eleven men besides himself who became twelve "eyewitnesses" to these plates. Their testimony is that they had "beheld and saw the plates and the engravings thereon" and that they "know of a surety that the said Smith has got the plates of which we have spoken." Now let's say this is all we know. Is it enough to believe? Before deciding we surely would want to personally ask them some questions and investigate their claims, just as we would want to personally talk to Paul's list of "witnesses." That's not unreasonable, just as we would doubt Balaam's tale until he made his ass talk in front of us (see Num. 22). In the case of the witnesses to Smith's gold plates, we know they were family, close friends, and/or his financial backers. We also know they didn't actually physically see these plates but rather saw them in visions and that some of them recanted later.[2]

When it comes to Paul's witnesses, most of the questions we need to know go unanswered. We do not know much about them except that it's likely they were probably all visionaries just like Paul. Besides, second-, third-, and fourth-hand testimony is simply not good enough. Perhaps they were duped. Did they all tell the same story? Did any of them recant? Without independent evidence to believe them, we must be skeptical.

We do not have anything written directly by Jesus himself or any of his original twelve disciples, nor do we have anything written by the Jewish leaders about Paul's claims, nor anything by the Romans. We have no records they were converted either. The Jews of Jesus's day believed in Yahweh and that he did miracles, and they knew their Old Testament prophecies. Yet overwhelming numbers of them did not believe Jesus was raised from the dead by Yahweh. So Christianity didn't take root in the Jewish homeland but had to reach out to the Greco Roman world for converts. Why should we believe if the Jews who were there didn't?

Furthermore, we have *no independent reports* that:

- the veil of the temple was torn in two when Jesus died (Mark 15:38);
- "darkness came over the whole land" (Mark 15:33) because "the sun stopped shining" (Luke 23:45);
- there was an earthquake at Jesus's death (Matt. 27:51–54) with another violent one the day he rose from the grave (Matt. 28:2);
- the saints were raised to life at his death and then waited until Sunday before walking out of their graves into Jerusalem, where they were seen by many people but never heard from again (Matt. 27:52–53).

Could these events really have happened without Philo, Josephus, rabbinic or Roman literature mentioning them? These silences are telling.

There is every reason to doubt Jesus rose from the dead.[3]

▶ Randal's Rebuttal

John suggests that Paul was an unreliable witness because he was prone to visions. Not only is this begging the question since it *assumes* that Paul's experiences had no divine cause, but it also doesn't explain the Damascus Road experience. It is one thing to have a vision; it is another thing to be knocked to the ground and set on a completely different life course.

Regardless, my argument relies on James, the leader whom Paul met for two weeks along with Peter (Gal. 1:18–19). It is very likely that Paul received the teaching summarized in 1 Corinthians 15:3–8 during this time. If John's argument is going to work, he can't simply raise a few doubts about Paul. He also has to explain the beliefs of Peter, the other early Christians, and of course James—not to mention the empty tomb. Unfortunately for John, naturalistic accounts of all the data end up looking even more miraculous than the miracle they're straining to avoid.

▶ John's Rebuttal

Just ask yourself what it would take for Joseph Smith's father and two brothers to believe him about the gold plates. They were visionaries, just like James was according to Paul, since he equated his visionary experience with the witnesses listed in 1 Corinthians 15:3–8. In a superstitious world like that, anything can be believed. It doesn't matter if James was a doubter before his vision, for a vision could easily change his mind in that world. And if Paul believed James's vision converted him, then he surely would have said so.

I have doubts James was a doubter. The only place we're told he doubted is an editorial comment in John 7:5: "For even his own brothers did not believe in him" (see vv. 2–5). How do we know the editor properly interpreted their words when the scholarly consensus is that the Gospel of John is a late and unreliable one? Eliminate it and there is nothing elsewhere indicating he doubted.

Nonetheless, if James was a nonbeliever prior to seeing the risen Jesus, then Jesus can convert people without abrogating their free will. If he can do this once with James, why doesn't he do this with others?

▶ Randal's Closing Statement

John's Mormon analogy breaks down because a golden plate isn't a resurrected person. While he is anxious to raise doubt about the credibility of witnesses, John cannot offer a satisfactory natural hypothesis to explain *all* the data, including the convictions of early Christians like James in the empty tomb and post-resurrection appearances.

▶ John's Closing Statement

It's not begging the question to doubt Joseph Smith's witnesses if all we know is that they saw the gold plates in visions. Paul said he had a vision on the Damascus road. It's related in Acts realistically as he saw it, since visionaries believe these things really happened.

◄ 20 ►

The Biblical God
Is an Incompetent Redeemer

Arguing the Affirmative: **JOHN THE ATHEIST**

Arguing the Negative: **RANDAL THE CHRISTIAN**

► John's Opening Statement

First look at J. L. Schellenberg's persuasive argument from divine hiddenness:

1. If there is a God, he is perfectly loving.
2. If a perfectly loving God exists, reasonable nonbelief does not occur.
3. Reasonable nonbelief occurs.
4. No perfectly loving God exists (from 2 and 3).
5. Hence, there is no God (from 1 and 4).[1]

If I have shown anything in this book, then I have a reasonable nonbelief. Therefore, unless someone can still maintain against the evidence that I don't have a reasonable nonbelief, Schellenberg's argument has been shown correct.

Now consider Theodore Drange's persuasive argument from unbelief for the existence of an evangelical God.

1. God wants all humans to believe before they die.
2. God can bring about that all, or almost all, humans believe before they die.
3. God always acts in accordance with what he most wants.
4. If God exists, all or almost all humans would believe before they die (from 1).
5. But not all humans believe before they die.
6. Therefore, God does not exist (from 2 and 3).[2]

Drange defends his argument from the free will defense, in part by arguing that if a person wants to believe the truth, then "for God to directly implant true beliefs into his/her mind would *not* interfere with, but would rather comply with, the person's free will." Drange argues that people "*want* to know the truth. They *want* to be shown how the world is really set up." So to perform miracles for them, as another option before God, "would only conform to or comply with that desire. It would therefore not interfere with their free will."[3] Drange defends his argument from the "Unknown-Purpose Defense" of God, in part by asking why God has chosen not to reveal his purpose for permitting nonbelief. "It would be in his interest to reveal that, for doing so would immediately destroy one main obstacle to people's belief in him," namely unbelief itself. "Thus, for God to keep his purpose secret is clearly counter-productive."[4]

Drange admits the *unknown-purpose* defense cannot be conclusively refuted. But we don't need to refute it. We just need to show that it's an improbable defense. It doesn't matter what the particular problem is for a person's faith. Having an omniscient God concept solves it. So believers must be convinced their faith is nearly impossible before they will consider it to be improbable, and that's an utterly unreasonable standard since we cannot hope to overcome this *omniscience escape clause*. Given that there are so many different faiths with the same escape clause, then believers should seriously consider that their own faith may equally be false. Sure, an omniscient God may exist (for the sake of argument), but how we judge whether he exists cannot rely over and over on his omniscience since that's exactly how other believers defend their own culturally inherited faith. Reasonable people must not have an unfalsifiable faith, and yet an omniscient concept of God makes one's faith basically unfalsifiable.

Are we really to believe this God exists when there is so much reasonable non-Christian belief in the world? Are we really to believe God chose a good era in human history to reveal himself, when it was clearly a barbaric, superstitious, prescientific one that later generations could easily discount as such? Are we really to believe God chose a good place to reveal himself in a remote part of the globe before the advent of global communications, such that our salvation depends on believing what these people said happened even though we were not there? Are we really to believe that non-Christian belief is a willful and damnable offense deserving punishment in hell (however conceived)? Does it not dawn on believers that overwhelming numbers of people simply accept and defend what they were raised to believe in their homes and cultures—that belief is overwhelmingly, if not completely, involuntary?

Christians themselves make most of my arguments for me since there are so many types of Christianities to choose from. Catholics offer cogent arguments against Protestants, who in turn offer cogent arguments against evangelicals, and so on. Christians also offer cogent arguments against the world religions, who in turn offer cogent arguments against Christianity. When they criticize each other they are *all* right. So I've rightly argued that believers ought to examine their own faith with the same level of skepticism they use when examining the other faiths in the *outsider test for faith*. Do it. What have you got to lose?

▶ Randal's Opening Statement

The 2002 British horror film *28 Days Later*, directed by Danny Boyle, depicts the dissolution of British society after a highly contagious virus called "rage" decimates the population. Imagine that you are a five-year-old living in London during the time the rage virus tears through the population. As you watch its effects unfolding in society, you witness the medical professionals working with the police, the military, and the European Centre for Disease Prevention and Control to control the pandemic. To begin with, they cordon off the roads into and out of the city, thereby cutting off your access to the outside world. How could it be that your supposed liberators are blocking the route to safety? Next, they begin separating those who have been exposed to the rage virus from those not yet exposed. Given your mother's early exposure, you find yourself and your father separated from her. This shocks you further, for your mother seemed fine to you. Finally, they initiate treatment of those exposed. You can hear your mother's screams as they inject her with a serum while she is quarantined. None of this makes sense to you. Things were bad before the so-called *liberators* arrived, but they weren't *this* bad. They blocked you in, took your mother, and are causing her great distress. Their actions strike you as utterly inexplicable and arbitrary.

Things look bad from the perspective of the five-year-old in the middle of an outbreak of rage. But things are very different from the perspective of those outside. We can readily see the logic of the medical, police, and military personnel as they work to contain and then treat the outbreak. They know much more about the pandemic and its proper treatment than you as a five-year-old know.

Christians believe that something like a rage virus infects the human race. They call it *original sin*. Theories as to its origin and the extent of the infection differ, but Christians agree that there is a universal infection, and you need not appeal to Adolf Hitler to find evidence of it. Consider a much more mundane example. In November 2006 comedian Michael Richards (who played the character of Cosmo Kramer on the sitcom *Seinfeld*) was being heckled by a couple of African-American gentlemen at the Laugh Factory comedy club in Los Angeles. Suddenly he exploded in retaliation, screaming a barrage of racist expletives and calling for a lynching. Unfortunately for Richards, somebody filmed the debacle and the footage quickly went viral. Shortly thereafter he appeared via satellite on David Letterman's show to offer an apology. Here are a couple excerpts from his rambling monologue:

> I'm really busted up over this and I'm very sorry to those people in the audience, the blacks, the Hispanics, the whites, everyone that was there that took the brunt of that anger and hate and rage and how it came through.
>
> For this to happen, for me to be on a comedy club and flip out and say this crap, you know I'm deeply, deeply sorry and, um, I've got, I'll get to the force-field of this hostility, why it's there why the rage is in any of us.[5]

As Richards spoke, he looked bewildered as though he was still in shock at his own abominable behavior, struggling to "get to the force-field of this hostility," to figure out "why the rage is in any of us." Paul had the same perplexity two millennia before: "I do not understand what I do. For what I want to do I do not do, but what I hate I do. . . . What a wretched man I am! Who will rescue me from this body that is subject to death?" (Rom. 7:15, 24).

What is this rage that infects us? What is it that allows creatures with such an unbounded potential for mercy, altruism, kindness, heroism, and love to have the potential for the most cruel, debased, malicious wickedness? How can it be that we are, as Pascal observed, simultaneously the glory and refuse of the universe?

We are all infected with rage. But God has moved in to deal with it through the death of his son, Jesus, and the work of his Spirit. We are but children in the city of the pandemic watching the forces move in to deal with the infection. At times the treatment may seem inexplicable and arbitrary. (How does the atonement work? Why did Christ have to die on a cross? How much cognitive information, if any, do people need to have about Christ to be saved by Christ?) But the fact that questions remain is no discredit to the liberators as they work to deliver us from the rage that hides in all of us.

▶ John's Rebuttal

The reason we sometimes act like brutes is because we evolved from them. There is therefore no need for atonement. It's who we are, and it's something that we alone can fix as morality evolves. The only reason Randal believes our rage (or sins) need atoning is because he was raised in a Western, Christianized culture. The vast majority of people in the world do not think someone like Jesus needs to be punished to death for the rest of us to be forgiven by a god. For instance, there is no sense in which punishment is related to forgiveness since we know of victims who have forgiven their attackers without it and other victims who will never forgive no matter how much they are punished. And it makes no sense at all to judge people based on whether they believe in the atoning death of Jesus, since belief is overwhelmingly involuntary at best.

Christians down through the centuries cannot agree on why Jesus needed to die for our sins. There are so many theories and counter-theories it can make our heads spin. Until theologians can come up with a coherent atonement theory, it's time to give up such a superstitious notion as a whole.

▶ Randal's Rebuttal

Let's focus on the second premise in Schellenberg's argument:

> 2. If a perfectly loving God exists, reasonable nonbelief does not occur.

There is a very good reason to think premise 2 is false and thus that the current nonbelief of many people is consistent with God's long-term plan to liberate human beings from original sin. Consider an analogy. Winston holds racist attitudes toward Indians, and he often shares his racist views with those he meets, including his neighborhood grocer Chahel. Little does Winston know that Chahel is himself an Indian. But if Chahel cares about Winston, shouldn't he reveal his identity? This can be put as follows:

> A. If a perfectly loving Chahel exists, Winston's reasonable nonbelief in Chahel's Indian identity does not occur.

In fact, A is false because Chahel could have very good reasons for keeping Winston ignorant of his true identity. For example, this may allow him to develop a deeper relationship with Winston so that when he finally does reveal his true identity Winston will be forced to rethink his racism more radically.

Schellenberg's premise 2 is false for the same reason. God could have excellent reasons for allowing nonbelief to persist in some people that are perfectly in accord with his redemptive plans for the world.

▶ John's Closing Statement

Once again the omniscience escape clause does the requisite work for Randal against the probabilities. Sure, it's a mere possibility that Randal is correct here, but so what? Probability is all that matters. To think God allows reasonable nonbelief when he could disallow it is reprehensible, since nonbelievers will be punished eternally for it.

▶ **Randal's Closing Statement**

John claims "there is no sense in which punishment is related to forgiveness" as though forgiveness is simply saying *sorry*. But forgiveness for a serious offense involves both repentance and reparations—an intentional stance to make amends. Through Christ, God offers reparations while seeking our repentance, and John has provided no reason to believe that God's redemptive work is "incompetent."

The Last Word

One day I decided to streamline the function of my computer by deleting all the old, useless files from the hard drive. But after I finished and restarted the computer I discovered, much to my chagrin, that not only had the operation not improved, it had noticeably worsened. In fact, my computer was no longer running properly at all. Slowly I realized that in my quest to streamline the computer's operation I had actually deleted a file that was essential to its proper running. Only after the fact did I realize that I would have to reinstall that file to regain the function of my computer.

God is like that file. Today many people think that by deleting God from their intellectual hard drive they have merely streamlined their worldview: Why have the world plus God when the world alone will suffice? God is just unnecessary baggage. Or so they think. Through these debates I have labored to show that this is actually a fundamentally mistaken assumption. Just as the file was essential to the proper running of the computer, so I have argued that God is essential to a proper understanding of the world. Consequently, if you delete God from your worldview, you suddenly find all sorts of other things disappearing as well—things that are very important for understanding the world correctly. Away goes any objective standard to judge a life well lived. Gone as well is any sense of an objective moral standard. So too we find objective beauty disappearing from view. We even lose any rational basis to hold that any of our beliefs are true. In our quest to streamline our worldview, we discover that the system no longer functions properly. It is a classic case of the cure being worse than the disease. Indeed, it turns out that the so-called disease *was* in fact the cure, and reinstallation of the file is the only solution.

John has been my unwitting partner in this exercise. His uncompromising defense of an atheistic worldview has been, I am glad to say, a clear and consistent presentation of the deflationary way a thinking atheist looks at the world. Just consider what he has conceded along the way. Relationships with other human beings are, in John's view, simply a way to bide our time in the house until we pass into the everlasting night. Truth is an unobtainable abstraction that is readily sacrificed on the pragmatic altar of survival (of our genes if not ourselves). And meaning joins beauty in a flickering marginal existence in the eye of the beholder.

The fact that John's perspective is so capably presented bears out my claim regarding the implications of atheism because John rejects every one of these things we value most. To be sure, he doesn't agree that his radical concessions defeat his worldview. On the contrary, he has tried a most implausible tactic by attempting to persuade us that all these things really don't matter. We don't *really* need the good, the true, and the beautiful. We can get by with the good *for us*, the true *for us*, and the beautiful *for us*. But this is false. If we know anything, we know that the good, the true, and the beautiful are objective values that exist above and beyond us as individuals and a species. Indeed, our innate orientation (despite John's asseverations to the contrary) to recognize them and in our better moments to live in accord with their objective facticity is a fundamental part of what makes us uniquely human.

From this perspective, John's advocacy of atheism is tantamount to the claim that we ought to reject civil government and all the benefits that go with it (roads, police, indoor plumbing, air conditioning) in favor of a bare, subsistence existence in the desert. Such a radical plea surely begs the question: What *reason* does John offer to take this radical step of deleting God, and all that goes with God, from our worldview? What *reason* does he have for us to abandon the benefits of civilized society in favor of a barren conceptual desert?

As best I can surmise, John seeks to offer both a general argument against theism and specific arguments against Christian theism. His first focus as expressed in this general argument really seems to take the form of a *force majeure* (a superior force) in which he suggests that intellectually honest, intelligent people simply cannot be theists. And what is the source of this *force majeure*? Apparently it is rooted in the advances of modern science generally and neo-Darwinism in particular. But this is mere bluster. We know this because countless highly educated individuals, including leading scientists and philosophers, maintain a robust and intellectually sophisticated theistic and Christian faith.[1] In fact, the intellectual reasons that drive academics to reject Christianity are philosophical, not scientific,[2] and these days that philosophy is typically naturalism.[3] But there is no good reason to accept naturalism (remember your mother's advice: "everyone else is doing it" is *not* a good reason). Indeed, as Alvin Plantinga has recently argued, while naturalism appears to have a superficial consonance with science, it is actually deeply incongruous with science.[4] And thus upon closer analysis it appears that John's cyclonic *force majeure* really has all the intensity of a light breeze barely glancing the ancient stone wall of a Gothic cathedral.

The second focus of John's attack is on Christian theism in particular. On this front he has taken on a range of topics in the Bible including child sacrifice, genocide, the role of women, and slaves. The idea, I presume, is that whatever a person may think of theism in general, Judeo-Christian theism is not possibly (or likely) to be true given the moral problems attendant to it. In each case I have labored to show that John's main arguments, even where they are successful, land only on the periphery of Christian conviction rather than at its heart. Admittedly some Christian readers may think I conceded too much at this point. Why not take on John's critique of the biblical case for matters like slavery or genocide more directly? I understand the sentiment and happily direct that disconsolate reader to the apologists who do engage in that enterprise.[5] But I'm not convinced that Christianity is well served by this kind of apologetic. Indeed, it seems to me that such an apologetic invites more problems than it solves.[6] And regardless, matters like biblical slavery and genocide surely are on the periphery of the gospel rather than at its pious heart, a place where we find cherished doctrines well worth defending—such as Trinity, incarnation, and atonement.

I want to stress that where Christianity is concerned I have not simply been on the defensive. On the contrary, I sought to defend not only the rational status of Christian faith commitments but also specific Christian beliefs in several particular areas including the experience of answered prayer and the evidence for the resurrection of Jesus. And so my goal has been not just to defend theism over-against atheism but to affirm Christian theism as the most intellectually satisfying view of the world.

So where does this leave us? If you're a Christian, I hope it leaves you sensing a certain vindication in your beliefs. There are excellent reasons to be a theist generally and a Christian theist in particular. There are not comparatively strong reasons to be an atheist. But what if you are at present an atheist? It may be at this moment that you're thinking there may be something more to theism than you thought. But perhaps you're not yet ready to commit to Christian theism. Perhaps it still requires you to believe more than you're able to accept at this time. So what do I suggest for you? Ask yourself if Christianity is a view of the world that you can accept *provisionally* as you seek to live in accord with the values that make us most fully human. If you find that you can take that step, then start doing so. Live *as if*

Christianity is true.[7] Begin exploring the rich intellectual and spiritual resources of the Christian tradition. Find a community of Christians with whom you can relate openly and honestly by sharing your beliefs and your doubts. Seek to live out the faith you do not yet fully possess through works of mercy and righteousness as you study, reflect, and learn. And then just see what happens. Most of all, never give up your tireless pursuit of that which none greater can be conceived.

Pax Christi,

Randal Rauser

▶ **Closing Thoughts from John**

I am honored that Dr. Rauser saw fit to consider me a worthy contender to argue against his faith. I consider him a worthy contender myself, and a friend. Kudos to him for initiating this book.

I have twin goals in co-writing this book. The first one is to force Christians to think about what they would believe if the Bible itself was undermined as a source of divine truth. My claim is that they probably won't believe at all. I'm trying to drive a wedge between the Bible and the brain of the believer. The second goal is to show in a cumulative fashion that Randal's God, having the three main attributes most Christians believe in today—omnibenevolence, omniscience, and omnipotence—does not exist. My focus is on the problem of evil for the believer, both with regard to God's supposed revelation in the Bible and his supposed actions in the world we see around us. You can see this from my ten chosen topics for debate (the even-numbered ones).

When it comes to defending his faith, all Randal can do is revert to special pleading, arguing from ignorance, and repeatedly punting to mere possibilities even though probabilities are all that matter. He also uses the *you too* fallacy, saying I have a

177

problem as an atheist too. The reason this is a fallacy is because there are just too many *you*'s to *too*. My arguments are the same ones Christian liberals use, and I quoted from them at times. Since they are believers, it does no good at all to say *you too* to them. Randal also cherry-picks the Bible in favor of his own moral intuitions and yet claims that when I share these same moral intuitions that mine are subjective. If mine are subjective, then so are his; or if my moral intuitions are sound ones, then so are his. He cannot have it both ways whenever we both reject certain biblical texts.

When it comes to the explanation of the whole shebang, we are faced with basically two options: (1) something—anything— has always existed, or (2) something—anything—popped into existence out of nothing. Either choice seems extremely un- likely—or possibly even absurd. There is little in our experience that can help us choose. But one of them is correct and the other is false. We either start with the brute fact that something has always existed or the brute fact that something popped into existence out of nothing. So the simpler our brute fact is then the more probable it is, per Ockham's razor. All that scientists have to assume is an equilibrium of positive and negative energy and the laws of physics. This is as close to nothing as science can get. But grant it and physicist Victor Stenger argues, "The probability for there being something rather than nothing can actually be calculated; it is over 60 percent." As such, "only by the constant action of an agent outside the universe, such as God, could a state of nothingness be maintained. The fact that we have something is just what we would expect if there is no God."[8]

By contrast, I find it implausible to believe that a Triune God (three persons in one):

- has always existed, considering the unlikelihood of even one eternal God-person;
- will forever exist, even though our entire experience is that everything has a beginning and an ending;

- exists as a fully formed being, even though our entire experience is that order grows incrementally;
- knows all true propositions, and consequently never learned any new ones;
- has all power, but doesn't exercise it like we would if we saw a burning child; and
- is present everywhere and knows what time it is everywhere in our universe, even though time is a function of movement and bodily placement.

How is it possible for this being to think or make choices or take risks (things that all involve weighing alternatives)? How could he have freely chosen who he is and what his values are, since there was never a previous time before he was who he is?

But let's grant that on each of Randal's ten chosen debate topics (the odd-numbered ones) he is correct. Let's grant first of all that there is a supernatural force (or being) out there who explains the whole shebang, gives life meaning, and is the basis for morality, reason, and beauty. I can grant all of these things and it would not make a difference. For at best all Randal can reasonably conclude with regard to God is that he existed at one time and then ceased to exist, or that he exists now but we cannot reasonably determine if he is a good God, a trickster God, or one who is watching us with enjoyment like rats in a maze to see what we conclude about it all. At best Randal's arguments lead us to a distant God, one who is indistinguishable from none at all—an unnecessary hypothesis we can simply do without.

In addition, even if this supernatural force (or being) answers prayers and raised Jesus from the dead, we still have no reasonable way of accepting these claims. Reasonable doubts abound for these claims such that thinking people cannot accept them. There are many claims that are true that reasonable people should not accept because of the lack of sufficient evidence. Surely there is a murderer whom no reasonable person suspects did the evil deed because there isn't sufficient evidence to think he did. Then too, perhaps someone really was abducted by aliens, but without sufficient evidence no reasonable person should accept his claim.

There is therefore no need to propose an alternative scenario to the resurrection hypothesis, just as a historian does not need to propose a different scenario after disputing what someone claimed happened at Custer's Last Stand. Perhaps there just isn't enough evidence to say for sure after having rejected it; although when it comes to the claim that Jesus resurrected, I did so in my book *Why I Became an Atheist*. What we do know is that incredible events happen all the time, like getting pregnant after a tubal ligation operation, meeting a twin brother on the street whom you never knew existed, or finding a bottle that had been at sea for five years washed up on your beachfront property. Accordingly, what's so hard about thinking something incredible happened that caused the early disciples to believe without punting to a miracle? I see no reason to think we should.

My claim is that the raw, uninterpreted historical data is simply not enough to believe God raised Jesus from the dead because there can be no relevant background knowledge or "priors" prior to concluding he did. The main reason Christians think the historical evidence for the resurrection is conclusive is because they have already come to believe in a God who did this particular miracle, and that's pretty much it. Overwhelming numbers of Jews in the days of Jesus did not believe it, along with millions of other people even after being confronted with this so-called evidence. One would think that if eternal damnation awaits someone who doesn't believe, then that evidence would be much stronger than it is. Since the evidence is weak, believers must continually punt to faith. But as I have argued, faith is not acceptable, especially when it comes to the historian's task.

Finally, let me comment on something that may not seem obvious but should. Randal has bypassed what I consider the proper protocol here. He has placed himself in the proverbial final championship game by jumping in line, as it were, bypassing other worthy religious contenders in order to debate me, an atheist. I have obliged him of course, but before debating an atheist he should have shown that his brand of Christianity can successfully win prior debate contests with the many other religionists found around the world—something he has not done. Why? Because the bottom line is that atheists are skeptics. That places us in a bracket all our own. We are not affirming anything. We are denying the claims of all religionists. We do not think there is sufficient evidence to believe in supernatural forces or beings. Since this is the case, religionists must determine among themselves who is their best contender to face off against us. That process did not happen here precisely because they cannot agree among themselves who should be in the finals.

In every part of the globe religionists who circumvent this proper protocol will have their provincial debates with atheists as if those are the only two options to consider: Hinduism versus atheism, or Islam versus atheism, or Orthodox Judaism versus atheism, or—well, you get the point. The implied assumption is that the culturally dominant religion gets to act like it has earned its place in the championship game simply by virtue of the fact that it is the dominant one. That is emphatically *not* the case.

If the proper protocol were followed, there wouldn't even be a final debate between a particular cultural religion and an atheist. That's because no religion can rise to the top by legitimately beating all the others. They would all just endlessly beat up on each other with no clear winners. And that's precisely one of the major reasons why we are atheists in the first place. It's because no religion can rightfully be shown to have any more epistemic warrant than the many others. They all share the same epistemic grounding; they all stand on the quicksand of a faith-based reasoning. So while I have granted Randal a place in the finals with me, now he must still go back and justify why he was here in the first place rather than one of the myriad numbers of other religions, including the various branches of his own.

All that believers must do is apply the same level of skepticism to their own religion as they do to the religions of others that they reject. This is what I call the *outsider test for faith*. When believers understand why they dismiss all other religions, they will understand why I dismiss theirs. If they refuse to do this, I merely ask them why the double standard? Why treat other religions differently than you do your own? Believers should be skeptical of what they were taught to accept given the proliferation of so many other religions and sects separated into distinct regions on the planet who learned their religion in the same way—on their mama's knee.

Be well,
John W. Loftus

Recommended Readings

Debate 1: If There Is No God, Then Life Has No Meaning

▶ *Randal's Recommended Readings*

Clark, Kelly James, ed., *Philosophers Who Believe: The Spiritual Journeys of 11 Leading Thinkers*. Downers Grove, IL: InterVarsity Academic, 1997.

Craig, William Lane, *Reasonable Faith*. 3rd ed. Wheaton: Crossway, 2008. Chap. 2.

Lewis, C. S., *Surprised by Joy: The Shape of My Early Life*. Rev. ed. New York: Houghton Mifflin Harcourt, 1995.

Morris, Thomas V. *Making Sense of It All: Pascal and the Meaning of Life*. Grand Rapids: Eerdmans, 1992.

▶ *John's Recommended Readings*

Antony, Louise M., ed. *Philosophers without Gods: Meditations on Atheism and the Secular Life*. Oxford: Oxford University Press, 2007.

Baier, Kurt, and Kai Nielsen. *The Meaning of Life*. Edited by E. D. Klemke. New York: Oxford University Press, 1981.

Martin, Michael. *Atheism, Morality, and Meaning*. Amherst, NY: Prometheus Books, 2002.

Debate 2: The Biblical Concept of God Evolved from Polytheism to Monotheism

▶ *John's Recommended Readings*

Day, John. *Yahweh and the Gods and Goddesses of Canaan.* Sheffield, UK: Sheffield Academic, 2002.

Friedman, Richard Elliot. *Who Wrote the Bible?* New York: Harper & Row, 1987.

Smith, Mark S. *The Origins of Biblical Monotheism: Israel's Polytheistic Background and the Ugaritic Texts.* Oxford: Oxford University Press, 2003.

Stark, Thom. "Yahweh's Ascendancy: Whither Thou Goest, Polytheism." *The Human Faces of God: What Scripture Reveals When It Gets God Wrong (and Why Inerrancy Tries to Hide It).* Eugene, OR: Wipf & Stock, 2011. Chap. 4.

▶ *Randal's Recommended Readings*

Enns, Peter. *Inspiration and Incarnation: Evangelicals and the Problem of the Old Testament.* Grand Rapids: Baker, 2005.

Padgett, Alan, and Patrick R. Keifert, eds. *But Is It All True? The Bible and the Question of Truth.* Grand Rapids: Eerdmans, 2006.

Sparks, Kenton. *God's Word in Human Words: An Evangelical Appropriation of Critical Biblical Scholarship.* Grand Rapids: Baker, 2008.

Debate 3: If There Is No God, Then Everything Is Permitted

▶ *Randal's Recommended Readings*

Hare, John. *God and Morality: A Philosophical History.* Malden, MA: Wiley-Blackwell, 2009.

———. *Why Bother Being Good? The Place of God in the Moral Life.* Eugene, OR: Wipf & Stock, 2010.

MacIntyre, Alasdair. *After Virtue: A Study in Moral Theory.* 3rd ed. Notre Dame: University of Notre Dame Press, 2007.

Quinn, Philip L. *Divine Commands and Moral Requirements.* Clarendon Library of Logic and Philosophy. New York: Oxford University Press, 1978.

▶ *John's Recommended Readings*

Epstein, Greg M. *Good without God: What a Billion Nonreligious People Do Believe.* New York: Harper, 2009.

Kurtz, Paul. *Forbidden Fruit: The Ethics of Humanism.* Amherst, NY: Prometheus Books, 1988.

Nielsen, Kai. *Ethics without God.* Rev. ed. Amherst, NY: Prometheus Books, 1990.

Shermer, Michael. *The Science of Good and Evil: Why People Cheat, Gossip, Care, Share, and Follow the Golden Rule.* New York: Henry Holt, 2004.

Singer, Peter. *How Are We to Live? Ethics in an Age of Self-Interest.* Amherst, NY: Prometheus Books, 1995.

Sinnott-Armstrong, Walter. *Morality without God?* Oxford: Oxford University Press, 2009.

Debate 4: The Biblical God Required Child Sacrifices for His Pleasure

▶ *John's Recommended Readings*

Levenson, Jon D. *The Death and Resurrection of the Beloved Son.* New Haven: Yale University Press, 1993.

Stark, Thom. "Making Yahweh Happy: Human Sacrifice in Ancient Israel." *The Human Faces of God: What Scripture Reveals When It Gets God Wrong (and Why Inerrancy Tries to Hide It).* Eugene, OR: Wipf & Stock, 2011. Chap. 5.

Stavrakopoulou, Francesca. *King Manasseh and Child Sacrifice: Biblical Distortions of Historical Realities.* Berlin: Walter de Gruyter, 2004.

▶ *Randal's Recommended Readings*

Kaiser, Walter C., Jr., Peter H. Davids, F. F. Bruce, and Manfred Brauch. *Hard Sayings of the Bible.* Downers Grove, IL: InterVarsity Academic, 1996.

McKnight, Scott. *A Community Called Atonement*. Nashville: Abingdon, 2007.

Smith, Christian. *The Bible Made Impossible: Why Biblicism Is Not a Truly Evangelical Reading of Scripture*. Grand Rapids: Brazos, 2011.

Debate 5: Science Is No Substitute for Religion

▶ *Randal's Recommended Readings*

Bouwsma, O. K. "Naturalism." *Journal of Philosophy* 45, no. 1 (1948): 12–22.

Collins, Francis S. *The Language of God: A Scientist Presents Evidence for Belief*. New York: Free Press, 2007.

Goetz, Stewart, and Charles Taliaferro. *Naturalism*. Grand Rapids: Eerdmans, 2008.

Lennox, John C. *God's Undertaker: Has Science Buried God?* London: Lion UK, 2009.

▶ *John's Recommended Readings*

Eller, David. "Is Religion Compatible with Science?" in *The Christian Delusion*, edited by John W. Loftus, chap. 11, 257–78. Amherst, NY: Prometheus, 2010.

Forrest, Barbara. "Methodological Naturalism and Philosophical Naturalism: Clarifying the Connection." http://www.infidels.org/library/modern/barbara_forrest/naturalism.html.

Stenger, Victor J. *God and the Folly of Faith: The Incompatibility of Science and Religion and Why It Matters*. Amherst, NY: Prometheus Books, 2012.

Debate 6: The Biblical God Commanded Genocide

▶ *John's Recommended Readings*

Niditch, Susan. *War in the Hebrew Bible: A Study in the Ethics of Violence*. Oxford: Oxford University Press, 1993.

Rowlett, Lori L. *Joshua and the Rhetoric of Violence: A New Historicist Analysis.* Sheffield, UK: Sheffield Academic, 1996.

Stark, Thom. "Blessing the Nations: Yahweh's Genocides and Their Justifications." *The Human Faces of God: What Scripture Reveals When It Gets God Wrong (and Why Inerrancy Tries to Hide It).* Eugene, OR: Wipf & Stock, 2011. Chap. 6.

———. *Is God a Moral Compromiser?* http://thomstark.net/copan /stark_copan=review.pdf.

———. "Review: Douglas S. Earl, *The Joshua Delusion? Rethinking Genocide in the Bible.*" http://religionatthemargins.com/2010 /11/the=joshua=delusion.

► *Randal's Recommended Readings*

Jenkins, Philip. *Laying Down the Sword: Why We Can't Ignore the Bible's Violent Verses.* New York: HarperOne, 2011.

Rauser, Randal. "'Let Nothing that Breathes Remain Alive': On the Problem of Divinely Commanded Genocide." *Philosophia Christi* 11, no. 1 (2009): 27–41. http://randalrauser.com/wp -content/uploads/2010/09/Rauser11.1.pdf.

———. *The Swedish Atheist, the Scuba Diver, and Other Apologetic Rabbit Trails.* Downers Grove, IL: InterVarsity, 2012. Chap. 22.

Seibert, Eric A. *Disturbing Divine Behavior: Troubling Old Testament Images of God.* Minneapolis: Fortress, 2009.

Wright, Christopher J. H. *The God I Don't Understand: Reflections on Tough Questions of Faith.* Grand Rapids: Zondervan, 2008. Chaps. 4–5.

Debate 7: God Is the Best Explanation of the Whole Shebang

► *Randal's Recommended Readings*

Collins, Robin. "The Teleological Argument: An Exploration of the Fine-Tuning of the Universe," in *The Blackwell Companion to Natural Theology*, edited by William Lane Craig and J. P. Moreland, 202–81. Malden, MA: Blackwell, 2009.

Craig, William Lane, and James D. Sinclair, "The *Kalam* Cosmological Argument," in *The Blackwell Companion to Natural*

Theology, edited by William Lane Craig and J. P. Moreland, 101–200. Malden, MA: Blackwell, 2009.

Pruss, Alexander R. "The Leibnizean Cosmological Argument," in *The Blackwell Companion to Natural Theology*, edited by William Lane Craig and J. P. Moreland, 24–100. Malden, MA: Blackwell, 2009.

▶ *John's Recommended Readings*

"The Fabric of the Cosmos: Universe or Multiverse?" *NOVA*, PBS, November 22, 2011.

Hawking, Stephen, and Leonard Mlodinow. *The Grand Design.* New York: Bantam Books, 2010.

Rundle, Bede. *Why There Is Something Rather than Nothing*. Oxford: Oxford University Press, 2006.

Stenger, Victor J. *God: The Failed Hypothesis*. Amherst, NY: Prometheus Books, 2007.

Debate 8: The Biblical God Does Not Care Much about Slaves

▶ *John's Recommended Readings*

Avalos, Hector. *Slavery, Abolitionism, and the Ethics of Biblical Scholarship*. Sheffield, UK: Sheffield Phoenix, 2011.

Douglass, Frederick. *My Bondage and My Freedom*. New York: Barnes & Noble Classics, 2005.

Finkelman, Paul. *Defending Slavery: Proslavery Thought in the Old South, A Brief History with Documents*. Boston: Bedford/St. Martin's, 2003.

▶ *Randal's Recommended Readings*

Haugen, Gary. *Just Courage: God's Great Expedition for the Restless Christian*. 2nd ed. Downers Grove, IL: InterVarsity, 2008.

Webb, William J. *Slavery, Women and Homosexuals: Exploring the Hermeneutics of Cultural Analysis*. Downers Grove, IL: InterVarsity Academic, 2001.

Wolterstorff, Nicholas. *Justice: Rights and Wrongs*. Princeton, NJ: Princeton University Press, 2010.

Debate 9: If There Is No God, Then We Don't Know Anything

▶ *Randal's Recommended Readings*

Alston, William P. *A Realist Conception of Truth*. Ithaca, NY: Cornell University Press, 1996. Chap. 8.

————. *The Reliability of Sense Perception*. Ithaca, NY: Cornell University Press, 1996.

Reppert, Victor. *C. S. Lewis's Dangerous Idea: In Defense of the Argument from Reason*. Downers Grove, IL: InterVarsity Academic, 2003.

Willard, Dallas. "Knowledge and Naturalism," in *Naturalism: A Critical Analysis*, edited by William Lane Craig and J. P. Moreland, 24–48. London: Routledge, 2000.

▶ *John's Recommended Readings*

Beversluis, John. "The Argument from Reason." *C S. Lewis and the Search for Rational Religion: Revised and Updated*. Amherst, NY: Prometheus Books, 2007. Chap. 6, pp. 143–94.

de Waal, Frans. *Primates and Philosophers: How Morality Evolved*. Princeton, NJ: Princeton University Press, 2006.

Griffin, Donald R. *Animal Minds*. Chicago: University of Chicago Press, 1992.

Hauser, Marc. *Moral Minds: How Nature Designed Our Universal Sense of Right and Wrong*. New York: Harper Perennial, 2007.

————. *Wild Minds: What Animals Really Think*. New York: Henry Holt, 2000.

Debate 10: The Biblical God Does Not Care Much about Women

▶ *John's Recommended Readings*

Coogan, Michael. *God and Sex: What the Bible Really Says*. New York: Twelve, 2010.

Newsom, Carol A., and Sharon H. Ringe, eds. *Woman's Bible Commentary: Expanded Edition with Apocrypha.* Louisville: Westminster John Knox, 1998.

Ranke-Heineman, Uta. *Eunuchs for the Kingdom of Heaven: Women, Sexuality and the Catholic Church.* Translated by Peter Heinegg. New York: Penguin, 1991.

Scholz, Susanne. *Sacred Witness: Rape in the Hebrew Bible.* Minneapolis: Fortress, 2010.

▶ *Randal's Recommended Readings*

James, Carolyn Custis. *Half the Church: Recapturing God's Global Vision for Women.* Grand Rapids: Zondervan, 2011.

Johnson, Elizabeth A. *She Who Is: The Mystery of God in Feminist Theological Discourse.* New York: Herder & Herder, 1993.

Jones, Serene. *Feminist Theory and Christian Theology.* Minneapolis: Fortress, 2000.

Debate 11: Love Is a Many Splendored Thing, but Only if God Exists

▶ *Randal's Recommended Readings*

King, Martin Luther, Jr. *Strength to Love.* Minneapolis: Fortress, 2010.

Lewis, C. S. *The Four Loves.* New York: Harcourt, Brace, 1960.

Outka, Gene. *Agape: An Ethical Analysis.* Princeton, NJ: Princeton University Press, 1977.

▶ *John's Recommended Readings*

Fisher, Helen. *Why We Love: The Nature and Chemistry of Romantic Love.* New York: Holt Paperbacks, 2004.

Lewis, Thomas, Fari Amini, and Richard Lannon. *A General Theory of Love.* New York: Vintage, 2001.

Sternberg, Robert, and Karin Weis, eds. *The New Psychology of Love.* New Haven: Yale University Press, 2006.

Debate 12: The Biblical God Does Not Care Much about Animals

▶ *John's Recommended Readings*

Loftus, John W. "The Bible and the Treatment of Animals." http://sites.google.com/site/thechristiandelusion/Home/the-bible-and-animals.

————. "The Darwinian Problem of Evil," in *The Christian Delusion*, edited by John W. Loftus, chap. 9, 237–70. Amherst: Prometheus, 2010.

Rachels, James. *Created from Animals: The Moral Implications of Darwinism*. Oxford: Oxford University Press, 1990.

Singer, Peter. *Animal Liberation*. New York, Harper Perennial, 2009.

▶ *Randal's Recommended Readings*

Alcorn, Randy. *Heaven*. Wheaton: Tyndale, 2004. Chaps. 39–40.

Halteman, Matthew C. *Compassionate Eating as Care of Creation*. HSUS Faith Outreach Booklet Series. Washington DC: HSUS, 2010. http://www.humanesociety.org/assets/pdfs/faith/compassionate_eating_halteman_book.pdf.

Linzey, Andrew. *Creatures of the Same God: Explorations in Animal Theology*. Brooklyn: Lantern Books, 2009.

Rauser, Randal. "Why Did God Create Carnivores?" Unpublished manuscript. http://randalrauser.com/wp-content/uploads/2011/06/1-Carnivores.pdf.

Webb, Stephen H. *On God and Dogs: A Christian Theology of Compassion for Animals*. New York: Oxford University Press, 2002.

Debate 13: Everybody Has Faith

▶ *Randal's Recommended Readings*

Plantinga, Alvin. *Warranted Christian Belief*. New York: Oxford University Press, 2000.

Rauser, Randal. *The Swedish Atheist, the Scuba Diver, and Other Apologetic Rabbit Trails.* Downers Grove, IL: InterVarsity, 2012. Chaps. 8–10.

————. *You're Not as Crazy as I Think: Dialogue in a World of Loud Voices and Hardened Opinions.* Colorado Springs: Biblica, 2011.

▶ *John's Recommended Readings*

Bering, Jesse. *The Belief Instinct: The Psychology of Souls, Destiny, and the Meaning of Life.* New York: W. W. Norton, 2011.

Boyer, Pascal. *Religion Explained: The Evolutionary Origins of Religious Thought.* New York: Basic Books, 2001.

Loftus, John W. *The Outsider Test for Faith: How to Know Which Religion Is True.* Amherst, NY: Prometheus Books, 2013.

Shermer, Michael. *The Believing Brain: From Ghosts and Gods to Politics and Conspiracies—How We Construct Beliefs and Reinforce Them as Truths.* New York: Times Books, 2001.

Stenger, Victor J. *God and the Folly of Faith: The Incompatibility of Science and Religion and Why It Matters.* Amherst, NY: Prometheus Books, 2012.

Debate 14: **The Biblical God Is Ignorant about Science**

▶ *John's Recommended Readings*

Carrier, Richard. "Christianity Was Not Responsible for Modern Science," in *The Christian Delusion*, edited by John W. Loftus, chap. 15, 396–419. Amherst, NY: Prometheus, 2010.

Coyne, Jerry A. *Why Evolution Is True.* New York: Viking Books, 2009.

Dawkins, Richard. *The Greatest Show on Earth: The Evidence for Evolution.* New York: Free Press, 2009.

▶ *Randal's Recommended Readings*

Brooke, John Hedley. *Science and Religion: Some Historical Perspectives.* Cambridge, UK: Cambridge University Press, 1991.

Hooykaas, R. *Religion and the Rise of Modern Science.* Vancouver: Regent College Publishing, 2000.

Lamoreux, Denis. *Evolutionary Creation: A Christian Approach to Evolution.* Eugene, OR: Wipf & Stock, 2008. Chaps. 4–7.

Walton, John H. *The Lost World of Genesis One: Ancient Cosmology and the Origins Debate.* Downers Grove, IL: InterVarsity Academic, 2009.

Debate 15: God Is Found in the Majesty of the Hallelujah Chorus

▶ *Randal's Recommended Readings*

Caldecott, Stratford. *Beauty for Truth's Sake: On the Re-enchantment of Education.* Grand Rapids: Brazos, 2009.

Markos, Louis. *Restoring Beauty: The Good, the True and the Beautiful in the Writings of C. S. Lewis.* Colorado Springs: Biblica, 2010.

Nichols, Aidan. *Redeeming Beauty: Soundings in Sacral Aesthetics.* Ashgate Studies in Theology, Imagination and the Arts. Aldershot, England: Ashgate, 2007.

▶ *John's Recommended Readings*

Carrier, Richard. "Natural Beauty." *Sense and Goodness without God: A Defense of Metaphysical Naturalism.* Bloomington, IN: Author House, 2005. Chap 5, pp. 349–66.

Dissanayake, Ellen. *Homo Aestheticus: Where Art Comes from and Why?* Seattle: University of Washington Press, 1995.

———. *What Is Art For?* Seattle: University of Washington Press, 1990.

Livingston, Margaret. *Vision and Art: The Biology of Seeing.* New York: Harry N. Abrams, 2002.

Debate 16: The Biblical God Is Ignorant about the Future

▶ *John's Recommended Readings*

Loftus, John W. "At Best Jesus Was a Failed Apocalyptic Prophet," in *The Christian Delusion*, edited by John W. Loftus, 316–43. Amherst, NY: Prometheus, 2010.

————. "Prophecy and Biblical Authority." *Why I Became an Atheist*. Rev. ed. Amherst, NY: Prometheus, 2012. Chap. 17.

————. "What We've Got Here Is a Failure to Communicate," in *The Christian Delusion*, edited by John W. Loftus, 181–206. Amherst, NY: Prometheus, 2010.

▶ *Randal's Recommended Readings*

Beilby, James K., and Paul R. Eddy, eds. *Divine Foreknowledge: Four Views*. Grand Rapids: InterVarsity Academic, 2001.

Bloom, John A. "Is Fulfilled Prophecy of Value for Scholarly Apologetics?" *Global Journal of Classical Theology* 1, no. 2 (1999). http://phc.edu/gj_prophesy.php.

Enns, Peter. *Inspiration and Incarnation: Evangelicals and the Problem of the Old Testament*. Grand Rapids: Baker, 2005. Chap. 4.

Debate 17: God Best Explains the Miracles in People's Lives

▶ *Randal's Recommended Readings*

Dembski, William. *The Design Inference: Eliminating Chance through Small Probabilities*. Cambridge Studies in Probability, Induction, and Decision Theory. Cambridge, UK: Cambridge University Press, 1998. Chap. 2.

Geivett, R. Douglas, and Gary R. Habermas. *In Defense of Miracles: A Comprehensive Case for God's Action in History*. Downers Grove, IL: InterVarsity Academic, 1997.

Rauser, Randal. *The Swedish Atheist, The Scuba Diver and Other Apologetic Rabbit Trails*. Downers Grove, IL: InterVarsity, 2012. Chap. 30.

▶ *John's Recommended Readings*

Schick, Theodore, Jr., and Lewis Vaughn. *How to Think about Weird Things: Critical Thinking for a New Age*. 6th ed. Boston: McGraw-Hill, 2010.

Stenger, Victor J. *God: The Failed Hypothesis*. Amherst, NY: Prometheus Books, 2007.

————. *Has Science Found God? The Latest Results in the Search for Purpose in the Universe*. Amherst, NY: Prometheus Books, 2003.

Debate 18: **The Biblical God Is an Incompetent Creator**

▶ *John's Recommended Readings*

Linden, David J. *The Accidental Mind: How Brain Evolution Has Given Us Love, Memory, Dreams, and God*. Cambridge, MA: Harvard University Press, 2007.

Marcus, Gary. *Kluge: The Haphazard Evolution of the Human Mind*. Boston: Mariner Books, 2009.

Coyne, Jerry. *Why Evolution Is True*. New York: Viking Books, 2009.

▶ *Randal's Recommended Readings*

Barbour, Ian G. *Religion and Science: Historical and Contemporary Issues*. New York: HarperOne, 1997.

Copan, Paul, and William Lane Craig. *Creation Out of Nothing: A Biblical, Philosophical and Scientific Exploration*. Grand Rapids: Baker Academic, 2004.

Craig, William Lane, and Quentin Smith, *Theism, Atheism and Big Bang Cosmology*. Oxford: Oxford University Press, 1993.

Flint, Thomas P. *Divine Providence: The Molinist Account*. Cornell Studies in the Philosophy of Religion. Ithaca, NY: Cornell University Press, 1998.

Debate 19: **Jesus Was Resurrected, So Who Do You Think Raised Him?**

▶ *Randal's Recommended Readings*

Craig, William Lane. *Reasonable Faith*. 3rd ed. Wheaton: Crossway, 2008. Chap. 8.

Habermas, Gary R., and Michael R. Licona. *The Case for the Resurrection of Jesus*. Grand Rapids: Kregel, 2004.

Licona, Michael R. *The Resurrection of Jesus: A New Historiographical Approach*. Downers Grove, IL: InterVarsity Academic, 2011.

Wright, N. T. *The Resurrection of the Son of God*. Vol. 3 of *Christian Origins and the Question of God*. Minneapolis: Fortress, 2003.

▶ *John's Recommended Readings*

Loftus, John W. "Did Jesus Bodily Rise from the Dead?" *Why I Became an Atheist*. 2nd ed. Amherst, NY: Prometheus, 2012. Chap. 20.

McCormick, Matthew S. *Atheism and the Case against Christ*. Amherst, NY: Prometheus Books, 2012.

Price, Robert M., and Jeffrey Jay Lowder. *The Empty Tomb: Jesus Beyond the Grave*. Amherst, NY: Prometheus Books, 2005.

Debate 20: The Biblical God Is an Incompetent Redeemer

▶ *John's Recommended Readings*

Drange, Theodore. *The Improbability of God*. Edited by Michael Martin and Rikki Monnier. Amherst, NY: Prometheus Books, 2006. Part 4.

Schellenberg, J. L. *Divine Hiddenness and Human Freedom*. Ithaca, NY: Cornell University Press, 1993.

———. *The Wisdom to Doubt: A Justification of Religious Skepticism*. Ithaca, NY: Cornell University Press, 2007.

▶ *Randal's Recommended Readings*

Cross, Richard. "Atonement without Satisfaction," in *Oxford Readings in Philosophical Theology*, Vol. 1 of *Trinity, Incarnation, Atonement*, edited by Michael Rea, 328–47. Oxford: Oxford University Press, 2009.

Heim, S. Mark. *Saved from Sacrifice: A Theology of the Cross*. Grand Rapids: Eerdmans, 2006.

Rauser, Randal. *Faith Lacking Understanding: Theology through a Glass Darkly*. Carlisle, UK: Paternoster, 2008. Chap. 5.

Swinburne, Richard. *Responsibility and Atonement*. Oxford: Oxford University Press, 1989.

Notes

Chapter 2

1. See Thom Stark, *The Human Faces of God: What Scripture Reveals When It Gets God Wrong (and Why Inerrancy Tries to Hide It)* (Eugene, OR: Wipf & Stock, 2011), 70–74.

Chapter 3

1. Robert Frost, "The Road Not Taken," in *Mountain Interval* (New York: Henry Holt and Company, 1920; Bartleby.com, 1999); online at www.bartleby.com/119/. Accessed August 8, 2012.

2. Richard Swinburne, *The Existence of God*, 2nd ed. (Oxford: Oxford University Press, 2004), 215.

Chapter 5

1. E. O. Wilson, *Consilience: The Unity of Knowledge* (New York: Vintage, 1999), 7.

2. Chet Raymo, *Skeptics and True Believers: The Exhilarating Connection between Science and Religion* (New York: Walker, 1998), 225 (emphasis added).

3. Ibid., 244, emphasis added.

4. Carl Sagan, *Pale Blue Dot: A Vision of the Human Future in Space* (New York: Ballantine Books, 1994), 300.

5. Ibid., 301.

Chapter 6

1. Douglas Earl, *The Joshua Delusion: Rethinking Genocide in the Bible* (Eugene, OR: Wipf & Stock, 2010).

Chapter 7

1. For a more precise definition of these two concepts, see Roderick Chisholm, *Person and Object: A Metaphysical Study* (London: George Allen & Unwin, 1976), 69–70.

2. Edward Tryon, "Is the Universe a Vacuum Fluctuation?" *Nature* (December 1973): 396–97; J. B. Hartle and Stephen Hawking "The Wave Function of the Universe," *Physical Review* (December 1983): 2960–75.

Chapter 8

1. Frederick Douglass, "Narrative of the Life of Frederick Douglass: An American Slave," in Maynard Mack, ed., *The Norton Anthology of World Masterpieces*, 6th ed. (New York: W. W. Norton, 1992), 729.

2. Hector Avalos, *Slavery, Abolitionism, and the Ethics of Biblical Scholarship* (Sheffield, UK: Sheffield Phoenix, 2011), 17.

3. Ibid., 64.

4. Ibid., 110.

5. William Wilberforce, *A Letter on the Abolition of the Slave Trade* (London: Luke Hansard and Sons, 1807), 318–19.

6. Ibid., 319. .

7. Rev. Dr. Martin Luther King Jr., "I Have a Dream," speech delivered August 28, 1963, Washington, DC; text online at *Chicago Tribune*, http://www.chicago tribune.com/news/nationworld/sns-mlk-ihaveadream,0,36081.story.

8. Stephen Tomkins, *William Wilberforce: A Biography* (Grand Rapids: Eerdmans, 2007).

9. Avalos, *Slavery, Abolitionism, and the Ethics of Biblical Scholarship*, 97–98.

10. Paul K. Jewett and Marguerite Shuster, *Who We Are: Our Dignity as Human: A Neo-Evangelical Theology* (Grand Rapids: Eerdmans, 1996), 166.

Chapter 9

1. This reflects Alvin Plantinga's argument from reason first developed in *Warrant and Proper Function* (Oxford: Oxford University Press, 1993) and most recently in *Where the Conflict Really Lies: Science, Religion, and Naturalism* (Oxford: Oxford University Press, 2009), chap. 10.

2. Richard Rorty, *Philosophical Papers, I, Objectivity, Relativism, and Truth* (Cambridge, UK: Cambridge University Press, 1991), 66.

3. I am indebted to Richard Carrier for many of the words and ideas interspersed here, including material from "Neither Life nor the Universe Appear Intelligently Designed," in *The End of Christianity*, John W. Loftus, ed. (Amherst, NY: Prometheus, 2011), 301 (used with permission).

4. See Frans de Waal, *Primates and Philosophers: How Morality Evolved* (Princeton: Princeton University Press, 2006), Marc Hauser, *Wild Minds: What Animals Really Think* (New York: Henry Holt, 2000), his *Moral Minds: How Nature Designed Our Universal Sense of Right and Wrong* (New York: Harper Perennial, 2007), and Donald R. Griffin *Animal Minds* (Chicago: University of Chicago Press, 1992).

Chapter 10

1. Michael Coogan, *God and Sex: What the Bible Really Says* (New York: Twelve, 2010), 24.

2. Ibid.

3. Quoted in Carol A. Newsom and Sharon H. Ringe, eds., *Woman's Bible Commentary: Expanded Edition with Apocrypha*. (Louisville: Westminster John Knox, 1998), 39.

4. Coogan, *God and Sex: What the Bible Really Says*, 25–26.

5. Ibid., 251.

6. Susanne Scholz, *Sacred Witness: Rape in the Hebrew Bible* (Minneapolis: Fortress, 2010), 185.

7. Quoted in Scholz, Ibid., 183.

8. Ibid., 184.

9. As translated in Coogan, *God and Sex*, 186.

10. Sojourner Truth, *Narrative of Sojourner Truth* (New York, 1853), 67.

11. Nell Irvin Painter, *Sojourner Truth: A Life, a Symbol* (New York: Norton, 1996), 4.

12. Corona Brezina, *Sojourner Truth's "Ain't I a Woman?" Speech* (New York: Rosen, 2005), 28–29.

Chapter 11

1. Andrew Brown, *The Darwin Wars* (London: Simon & Schuster, 1999), 1.

2. Ibid., 2 (emphasis added).

3. Lorne Campbell and Bruce J. Ellis, "Commitment, Love and Male Retention," in *The Handbook of Evolutionary Psychology*, ed. David M. Buss (Hoboken, NJ: Wiley, 2005), 420.

4. See William Hasker, "Evolution and Alvin Plantinga," *Perspectives on Science and Christian Faith* 44 (1992): 158.

5. Konrad Lorenz, *King Solomon's Ring* (New York: Crowell, 1952), 158–59.

6. On love in general, see Robert Sternberg and Karin Weis, eds., *The New Psychology of Love* (New Haven, CT: Yale University Press, 2006); Helen Fisher, *Why We Love: The Nature and Chemistry of Romantic Love* (New York: Holt Paperbacks, 2004); Thomas Lewis, Fari Amini, and Richard Lannon, *A General Theory of Love* (New York: Vintage, 2001).

7. Christopher Hitchens, *The Missionary Position: Mother Teresa in Theory and Practice* (New York: Verso, 1995).

Chapter 12

1. Andrew Linzey, *Why Animal Suffering Matters* (Oxford: Oxford University Press, 2009), 47.

2. Ibid., 35.

3. I have written somewhat extensively on this topic. See John W. Loftus, *Why I Became an Atheist*, 2nd ed. (Amherst, NY: Prometheus, 2012), chaps. 11–12; and see John W. Loftus, ed., *The Christian Delusion* (Amherst, NY: Prometheus, 2010), chap. 9. See especially an essay titled "The Bible and the Treatment of Animals"

on the official website for *The Christian Delusion*, http://sites.google.com/site/thechristiandelusion/Home/the-bible-and-animals.

4. Richard Dawkins, *River Out of Eden: A Darwinian View of Life* (New York: Basic Books, 1996), 95–96.

5. See C. S. Lewis's discussion in *The Problem of Pain* (New York: MacMillan, 1944), 136.

Chapter 13

1. *Religulous*, directed by Larry Charles (Santa Monica, CA: Lions Gate Entertainment, 2008), DVD.

2. Richard Dawkins, *The God Delusion*, 2nd ed. (Boston: Mariner, 2008), 45.

3. John W. Loftus, "Faith Is Equivalent to Irrationality," *Debunking Christianity*, at http://debunkingchristianity.blogspot.com/2010/09/faith-is-equivalent-to-irrationality.html.

4. William Kingdon Clifford, "The Ethics of Belief," in *Lectures and Essays*, vol. 2 (n.p.: MacMillan, 1879), 186.

5. Anthony Kenny, *What Is Faith? Essays in the Philosophy of Religion* (Oxford: Oxford University Press, 1992), 6.

6. Michael Shermer, *The Believing Brain: From Ghosts and Gods to Politics and Conspiracies—How We Construct Beliefs and Reinforce Them as Truths* (New York: Times Books, 2001), 5.

7. Jesse Bering, *The Belief Instinct: The Psychology of Souls, Destiny, and the Meaning of Life* (New York: W. W. Norton, 2011), 36.

8. Pascal Boyer, *Religion Explained: The Evolutionary Origins of Religious Thought* (New York: Basic Books, 2001).

Chapter 14

1. Neil DeGrasse Tyson, "Holy Wars," in *Science and Religion: Are they Compatible?* Paul Kurtz, ed. (Amherst, NY: Prometheus, 2003), 74–75.

2. See chapter 5 in Loftus, *Christian Delusion*, 109–47.

3. Loftus, *Why I Became an Atheist*, 276–77.

4. Richard Carrier has argued in *The Christian Delusion*, that the Christian apologists' claim that their faith produced modern science is "false in every conceivable detail," 397.

Chapter 15

1. Richard Dawkins, *Climbing Mount Improbable* (New York: Norton, 1996), 256.

2. Ibid.

Chapter 16

1. The book of Haggai concludes (2:20–23) "with a strongly worded hope centered on Zerubbabel as the divinely chosen Davidic leader, the 'servant,' the 'signet ring,' royal executive of God." Paul J. Achtemeier, Harper's Bible Dictionary (San Francisco: Harper & Row, 1985), 366.

2. See Loftus, *Why I Became an Atheist*, chap. 17.

3. Robert J. Miller, *Born Divine: The Births of Jesus and Other Sons of God* (Santa Rosa, CA: Polebridge, 2003), 173.

4. C. F. D. Moule, *The Origin of Christology* (Cambridge, UK: Cambridge University Press, 1977), 129.

5. See chapter 12 in Loftus, *Christian Delusion*, 316–43.

6. As I argued in *Christian Delusion*, chap. 7, 181–206.

Chapter 17

1. Cited in Frank Wade, *Transforming Scripture* (New York: Church Publishing, 2008), 39.

2. See William Dembski, *The Design Inference: Eliminating Chance through Small Probabilities*, Cambridge Studies in Probability, Induction and Decision Theory (Cambridge, UK: Cambridge University Press, 1998), chap. 2.

3. See Victor J. Stenger's *Has Science Found God? The Latest Results in the Search for Purpose in the Universe* (Amherst, NY: Prometheus Books, 2003), and his *God: The Failed Hypothesis* (Amherst, NY: Prometheus Books, 2007), 94–102. The one case that showed otherwise turned out to be completely unreliable, or even a fraud. See Dr. Bruce Flamm, "The Columbus University Miracle Study," in *Science Under Siege: Defending Science, Exposing Pseudoscience*, Kendrick Frazier, ed., (Amherst, NY: Prometheus Books, 2009).

4. John Allen Paulos, *Innumeracy* (New York: Hill and Wang, 1988), 24.

5. Matt McCormick, "The Salem Witch Trials and the Evidence for the Resurrection," in Loftus, *End of Christianity*, 395n2.

6. Herbert Benson, Jeffery A. Dusek, Jane B. Sherwood, Peter Lam, et al. "Study of the Therapeutic Effects of Intercessory Prayer (STEP) in Cardiac Bypass Patients: A Multicenter Randomized Trial of Uncertainty and Certainty of Receiving Intercessory Prayer," *American Heart Journal* 151, no. 4 (2006): 934–42.

Chapter 18

1. Sam Harris, *Letter to a Christian Nation* (New York: Knopf, 2006), 78.

2. David J. Linden, *The Accidental Mind, How Brain Evolution Has Given Us Love, Memory, Dreams, and God* (Cambridge, MA: Harvard University Press, 2007), 240, 242. A Rube Goldberg contraption is an unnecessarily complex machine that performs a very simple task.

3. Gary Marcus, *Kluge: The Haphazard Evolution of the Human Mind* (Boston: Mariner Books, 2009), 2.

4. Ibid., 1.

Chapter 19

1. Josepheus, *Antiquities*, bk. 20, chap. 9.

2. On this see David Persuitte, *Joseph Smith and the Origins of the Book of Mormon*, 2nd ed. (Jefferson, NC: McFarland, 2000).

3. For a much more extensive treatment, see Loftus, *Why I Became an Atheist*, chap. 12.

Chapter 20

1. J. L. Schellenberg, *Divine Hiddenness and Human Freedom* (Ithaca, NY: Cornell University Press, 1993), 83. See also his book *The Wisdom to Doubt: A Justification of Religious Skepticism* (Ithaca, NY: Cornell University Press, 2007).

2. This is a truncated version of Drange's argument seen in part 4 of Michael Martin and Rikki Monnier, eds., *The Improbability of God* (Amherst, NY: Prometheus Books, 2006), 337–79.

3. Ibid., 350 (emphasis in original).

4. Ibid, 353.

5. Michael Richards on *The Late Show with David Letterman*, CBS, November 20, 2006; video clip "Michael Richards Apology on Letterman," available online at http://www.youtube.com/watch?v=IwBoVZh1ruQ (accessed September 27, 2012).

The Last Word

1. On the faith of scientists, see the much cited study by Edward Wilson and Larry Witham, "Scientists Are Still Keeping the Faith," *Nature* 386 (April 1997): 435–36. On the faith of philosophers, read atheist philosopher Quentin Smith's lament over the resurgence of theism (and Christian theism) within academic philosophy in "The Metaphilosophy of Naturalism," *Philo*, 4, no. 2 (2001), 195–215.

2. Needless to say there are many nonintellectual factors (e.g., personal, social, economic) that also form the beliefs of individuals—scientists included—but these factors are of no rational or evidential value.

3. See Bruce L. Gordon and Bruce A. Dembski, eds., *The Nature of Nature: Examining the Role of Naturalism in Science* (Wilmington, DE: ISI Books, 2011). Another common philosophical obstacle is pluralism, for which see Alvin Plantinga, *Warranted Christian Belief* (Oxford: Oxford University Press, 2000), chap. 13. John Loftus has argued for atheism based on the plurality of religious perspectives in his "outsider test of faith." I have responded to his test in Randal Rauser, *The Swedish Atheist, the Scuba Diver and Other Apologetics Rabbit Trails* (Downers Grove, IL: InterVarsity, 2012), chap. 6.

4. Alvin Plantinga, *Where the Conflict Really Lies: Science, Religion, and Naturalism* (New York: Oxford University Press, 2011). See also Michael Rea, *World without Design: The Ontological Consequences of Naturalism* (New York: Oxford University Press, 2004).

5. See, for instance, Paul Copan, *Is God a Moral Monster? Making Sense of the Old Testament God* (Grand Rapids: Baker, 2011).

6. For a critique of Copan, *Is God a Moral Monster?* see Thom Stark, *Is God a Moral Compromiser? A Critical Review of Paul Copan's "Is God a Moral Monster?"* online at http://religionatthemargins.com/2011/07/the-real-second-edition-is-god-a-moral-compromiser-a-critical-review-of-paul-copans-is-god-a-moral-monster/.

7. See Rauser, *The Swedish Atheist, the Scuba Diver, and Other Apologetic Rabbit Trails*, chaps. 31–32.

8. Victor Stenger, *God: The Failed Hypothesis*, 132–33. See also Stenger's *The Comprehensible Cosmos: Where Do the Laws of Physics Come From?* (Amherst, NY: Prometheus Books, 2006), supplement H.

John W. Loftus is a former Christian minister and apologist with degrees in philosophy, theology, and the philosophy of religion from Lincoln Christian University and Trinity Evangelical Divinity School. He also did PhD studies at Marquette University in theology and ethics. John is the founder of an influential blog called *Debunking Christianity* (http://debunkingchristianity. blogspot.com/). He is the author of *Why I Became an Atheist: A Former Preacher Rejects Christianity* and *The Outsider Test for Faith: How to Know Which Religion Is True*. He is also the editor of *The Christian Delusion: Why Faith Fails* and *The End of Christianity*. He lives in Indiana.

Randal Rauser (MCS, Regent College; PhD, King's College London) is associate professor of historical theology at Taylor Seminary, Edmonton, Canada. He is the author of several books, including *Finding God in* The Shack, *You're Not as Crazy as I Think*, and *The Swedish Atheist, the Scuba Diver, and Other Apologetic Rabbit Trails*. He is a popular speaker and gifted communicator who seeks to bring the truth of Scripture to bear on the real-life issues of today and who blogs regularly at www. randalrauser.com. He lives in Alberta.